生态文明教育中学校本课程
Middle-school Based Curriculum on Ecological Civilization Education

中国野生动物保护

Wildlife Protection in China

中国绿色碳汇基金会
北京第二外国语学院附属中学 编写

China Green Carbon Foundation
The High School Affiliated to Beijing International Studies University

科学普及出版社
·北京·

图书在版编目（CIP）数据

中国野生动物保护：汉英对照 / 中国绿色碳汇基金会，北京第二
外国语学院附属中学编写 . — 北京：科学普及出版社 . 2017.11
生态文明教育中学校本课程
ISBN 978-7-110-09216-3

Ⅰ. ①中⋯ Ⅱ. ①中⋯ ②北⋯ Ⅲ. ①野生动物－保护－中国－
中学－课外读物－汉、英 Ⅳ. ① G634.73

中国版本图书馆 CIP 数据核字 (2015) 第 177102 号

策划编辑　徐扬科
责任编辑　王　珅
责任校对　杨京华
责任印制　徐　飞
装帧设计　北京市青少年音像出版社设计部

出　　版　科学普及出版社
发　　行　中国科学技术出版社发行部
地　　址　北京市海淀区中关村南大街 16 号
邮　　编　100081
发行电话　010–63583170
传　　真　010–62173081
投稿电话　010–62176522
网　　址　http://www.cspbooks.com.cn

开　　本　787mm × 1092mm　1/16
字　　数　390 千字
印　　张　10.5
版　　次　2017 年 11 月第 1 版
印　　次　2017 年 11 月第 1 次印刷
印　　刷　廊坊飞腾印刷包装有限公司

书　　号　ISBN 978–7–110–09216–3/G・3855
定　　价　30.00 元

（凡购买本社图书，如有缺页、倒页、脱页者，本社发行部负责调换）

编 委 会
Editorial Board

主　任 李怒云　付晓洁
Directors　　Li Nuyun, Fu Xiaojie

副主任 苏宗海　李　果
Deputy Directors　Su Zonghai, Li Guo

主　编 陈建伟　金　崑　王维胜　周丽红　薛　唱
Chief Editors　Chen Jianwei, Jin Kun, Wang Weisheng, Zhou Lihong, Xue Chang

编　委 袁金鸿　林花苗　黄英玉　赵红梅　李海燕　张　颖
Editorial Board Members　Yuan Jinhong, Lin Huamiao, Huang Yingyu, Zhao Hongmei, Li　Haiyan, Zhang Ying

序　言
Foreword

　　我国地域辽阔、地貌复杂、河流纵横、湖泊众多、气候多样，为各种生物及生态系统类型的形成与发展提供了优越的自然条件，从而成为世界上野生动物多样性极为丰富的国家之一。由于我国大部分地区未受到第三纪和第四纪大陆冰川的影响，因而保存有大量的特有物种。大熊猫、川金丝猴、滇金丝猴、黔金丝猴、华南虎、藏羚、白唇鹿、海南坡鹿、褐马鸡、绿尾虹雉、白鱀豚、扬子鳄等均为我国特有的珍稀濒危野生动物，其中的大熊猫更是举世闻名，深受全世界人民喜爱。

China is characterized by vast territory, complex topography, crisscrossed rivers, numerous lakes, and diverse climates, providing superior natural conditions for formation and development of a variety of creatures and types of ecosystems and thus becoming one of the countries with the richest wildlife diversity in the world. Because most parts of China were not affected by the tertiary and quaternary continental glacier, a large number of endemic species are preserved. *Aiuropoda melanoleuca, Rhinopithecus roxellanae, Rhinopithecus bieti, Rhinopithecus brelichi, Panthera tigris amoyensis, Pantholops hodgsonii, Cervus albirostris, Cervus eldii, Crossoptilon manchuricum, Lophophorus lhuysii, Lipotes vexillifer,* and *Alligor sinensis* are all unique rare and endangered wild animals in China. Among them, *Aiuropoda melanoleuca* is world famous and loved by people around the world.

　　野生动物是自然生态系统的重要组成部分，与人类的生存和发展息息相关。野生动物是人类在自然界中的同伴，保护野生动物就是保护人类自身。随着人类社会的不断发展，野生动物资源受到了严重威胁，引起国际社会广泛关注。在人口增长、社会经济快速发展的背景下，野生动物及其栖息地仍受到环境污染、森林砍伐、土地开垦和非法贸易等多种因素的威胁，迫切需要采取进一步的措施强化保护。各国政府都采取了相应措施，保护野生动物及其栖息环境，合理开发和利用野生动物资源。

Wildlife is an important component of the natural ecosystem and is closely related with human survival and development. Wildlife is a fellow of human beings in nature and protecting wildlife is protecting human beings. With the continuous development of human society, wildlife resources are seriously threatened, causing widespread concern in the international community. Under the background of population growth and rapid socio-economic development, wildlife and its habitats are still subject to threats from a variety of factors like environmental pollution, deforestation, land reclamation, and illegal trade. Further measures are in urgent need to strengthen the protection. Governments from different countries have taken appropriate measures to protect wildlife and its habitats and to rationally develop and utilize wildlife resources.

　　当前，我国野生动物保护事业正在进入良性发展阶段。我国政府高度重视野生动物保护工作，先后加入了《濒危野生动植物种国际贸易公约》《生物多样性公约》，相继颁布了《中华人民共和国森林法》《中华人民共和国野生动物保护法》《中华人民共和国陆生野生动物保护实施条例》等一系列法律法规及多项行政规章；建立了数量众多的自然保护区，使野生动物尤其是珍稀濒危野生动物得到了保护；通过开展日常监管和组织专项执法行动，打击破坏野生动物资源的犯罪行为；积极加强野生动物繁育工作，最大限度地保护野生动物资源；连续多年组织开展宣传教育活动，提高人们爱护自然、保护野生动物的意识；积极开展国际野生动物保护和科研交流，参与国际相关保护行动。当前，我国正在全力推进生态文明建设，野生动物保护是其中重要内容之一，生态文明建设为保护自然生态和野生动物提供了强有力的保障。

Currently, the cause of wildlife protection in China is entering a virtuous development stage. Chinese government attaches great importance to the protection of wildlife by joining *Convention on International Trade in Endangered Species of Wild Fauna and Flora* and *Convention on Biological Diversity*, and has promulgated a series of laws and regulations and a number of administrative rules such as *Forest Law of the People's Republic of China*, *Law of the People's Republic of China on the Protection of Wildlife*, and *The Terrestrial Wildlife Implementation Regulation of the People's Republic of China*. The government has also established a large number of nature reserves to protect wildlife, especially rare and endangered wild animals; it has undertaken daily supervision and organized special enforcement actions against the crime that destructs wildlife resources; it has been actively working to strengthen the breeding of wildlife and maximize the protection of wildlife resources; the government has also organized educational campaigns to raise people's awareness of loving nature and protecting wildlife for consecutive years and has actively carried out international wildlife conservation and research exchanges and participated in relevant international protection actions. At present, China is promoting the construction of ecological civilization with all its strength, and wildlife protection is one important part of it. The development of ecological civilization provides a strong guarantee to protect natural ecosystem and wildlife.

　　有关部门组织编写了《中国野生动物保护》一书，这是一项十分有意义的工作。该书的内容十分丰富，科学性强、科普性强。在此，我希望，全社会和每个人，尤其是中学生朋友们都从我做起，做到不滥食野生动物，发现乱捕、滥猎、非法经营野生动物的不法行为，要向有关部门积极举报；做文明旅行者，不恐吓野生动物，不污染、不破坏野生动物的栖息环境；积极学习和宣传野生动物保护科普知识，促进人类与野生动物和谐相处；积极参与并倡导身边的亲人、朋友共同参与野生动物保护公益行动，为保护野生动物做出贡献。祝中学生朋友们学习进步、健康成长，将来成为建设祖国的栋梁！

Competent authorities organized the edition of *Wildlife Protection in China*, which was a very meaningful work. The book includes rich and scientific content. Here, I hope that the whole society and individuals, especially middle school students, can take the initiative not to eat wildlife and be bold to report to the competent authorities when they find unauthorized predation, excessive hunting, or illegal trade of wildlife; I hope they can be civilized travelers who do not intimidate wildlife, or pollute and destroy the habitats of wildlife; I hope they can be active in learning and promoting wildlife protection knowledge and promote harmony between humans and wildlife; I hope they can actively participate in and convince their relatives and friends of participating in public activities designed to protect wildlife and make contributions to the protection of wildlife. I wish middle school students to make progress in their studies and grow up healthily to be pillars of the motherland!

中国工程院院士　东北林业大学野生动物资源学院教授　　马建章

Academician of the Chinese Academy of Engineering and
Professor of College of Wildlife Resources in Northeast
Forestry University

Ma Jianzhang

2014 年 7 月 28 日

July 28, 2014

前　言
Preface

　　为了启发广大中学生对野生动物保护知识的了解和兴趣，唤起他们对大自然和对祖国的热爱，进而推动青少年生物科技活动更加广泛地开展，吸引更多的人从小关心生态和环境，特别是关心野生动物保护等全人类共同关注的重大课题，中国绿色碳汇基金会、北京第二外国语学院附属中学组织有关专家及教师编写了《中国野生动物保护》教材。这本教材涵盖了野生动物保护基础理论知识、我国野生动物多样性、我国野生动物保护措施、我国野生动物保护取得的成就、我国野生动物保护工作面临的挑战、保护野生动物——中学生在行动等内容。

In order to inspire the middle school students to understand and develop interest in wildlife protection, arouse their love for nature and the motherland, and thus promote wide hosting of biotech activities for the young and attract more people to be concerned about ecology and the environment since young, especially about wildlife protection and other major issues of common concern of mankind, China Green Carbon Foundation and the High School Affiliated to Beijing International Studies University organized experts and teachers to write *Wildlife Protection in China*. This textbook covers the basic theoretical knowledge of wildlife protection, wildlife diversity, wildlife protection measures, achievements and challenges in wildlife protection, and protection of wildlife — actions from middle school students in China.

　　希望中学生朋友们热爱自然，努力学习科学知识，探索野生动物奥秘，保护野生动物，维护生态平衡，在德、智、体、美、劳等各方面健康成长，为将来建设美丽中国贡献自己的力量。

We hope that middle school students will love nature, learn scientific knowledge, explore the mysteries of wildlife, protect wildlife, maintain ecological balance, grow up healthily in moral, intellectual, physical, aesthetic, and community service aspects, and contribute to the development of China.

　　感谢国家林业局野生动植物保护与自然保护区管理司总工程师严旬博士为本书提出宝贵意见。

Thanks Dr. Yan Xun, the chief engineer of the State Forestry Administration for putting forward valuable suggestions for the book.

编　者
Editors

目　录
Table of Contents

第一章 走近野生动物
Chapter I Approaching Wildlife

动物是一个尽人皆知的概念，是地球生态系统的重要组成部分。你知道什么是野生动物吗？它与家养动物又有什么区别呢？本章开始，我们共同走近野生动物，了解野生动物的特征与分布，认识一下我国的野生动物。

Animal is a well-known concept. It is an important component of the ecosystem of the Earth. Do you know what wildlife is? What's the difference between wildlife and domestic animals? From this chapter, we will approach wildlife to understand the characteristics and distribution of wildlife and learn about them in our country.

第一节 野生动物的特征与分布
Section I Characteristics and Distribution of Wildlife

你知道吗？
Do you know?

野生动物是指凡生存在天然自由状态下，或来源于天然自由状态虽经短期饲养但还没有产生变异的各种动物。但是，家畜或家禽走失或被放归到野外，即使能够独立生存，也不能称为野生动物。例如家骆驼走失到野外，即使独立存活了几十年也不能称作野生动物。

Wildlife refers to various kinds of animals that live in a natural state or come from a natural state, but have not undergone evolutionary change in spite of having short term feeding. However, livestock or poultry, that is lost or released into the wild, is not considered as wildlife, even if they can survive independently. For example, a home-raised camel, that is lost in the wild, cannot be regarded as wildlife even if it has survived independently for decades.

一、野生动物的特征
I. Characteristics of Wildlife

野生动物一般在野外生长繁殖。它们或独立地游走于栖息地，或成群结伴地定居、捕食、迁移、繁殖，在广袤的大自然中寻找着属于它们的生存空间。因此，野生动物一般具有不依靠人类饲喂而在野外独立生存、可繁殖的种群等特征。野生动物生存的三大要素是食物、水和隐蔽地。

Wildlife usually grows and reproduces in the wild. They walk independently in habitats, or settle, prey, migrate, and reproduce in group, looking for living space of their own in the vast nature. Therefore, wildlife does not rely on the feeding of humans but survives independently in the wild, with the characteristic of population fecundity. The three elements for the survival of wildlife are food, water and shelter.

二、我国野生动物的地理分布
II. Geographical Distribution of Wildlife in China

从动物地理角度，我国动物区系区分为两个界、七个区。两个界为古北界和东洋界。七个区为东北区、华北区、蒙新区、青藏区（属古北界），以及西南区、华中区、华南区（属东洋界）。

From the perspective of zoogeography, the fauna in China is divided into two realms and seven regions. The two realms are for the Palaearctic Realm and Oriental Realm, while the seven regions are Northeast Region, North China Region, Inner Mongolia-Xinjiang Region and Qinghai-Tibet Region (belonging to the Palaearctic Realm), and Southwest Region, Central China Region, and South China Region (belonging to the Oriental Realm).

（一）古北界
(I) Palaearctic Realm

1. 东北区
1. Northeast Region

东北区包括大兴安岭、小兴安岭、张广才岭、老爷岭、长白山地和松辽平原。陆栖脊椎动物各纲中的东北型，分布区多在区内相互重叠。主要代表种有黑龙江林蛙、中国林蛙、黑龙江草蜥、团花锦蛇、细嘴松鸡、丹顶鹤、东北兔和紫貂等。北方型的代表种有极北小鲵、胎生蜥蜴、柳雷鸟、攀雀、雪兔、驼鹿、驯鹿、狍、狼等。

It includes Great Khingan, Lesser Khingan, the Zhangguangcai Mountains, the Laoye Mountains, the Changbai Mountains, and the Songliao Plain. The Northeast China native animals in terrestrial vertebrates are mostly distributed in overlapping zones in the regions. The main representatives are *Rana amurensis*, *Rana cheninensis*, *Takydromus amurensis*, *Elaphe davudi*, *Tetrao parvirostris*, *Grus japonensis*, *Lepus mandshuricus*, and *Martes zibelina*. The representatives to northern China include *Salamandrella keyserlingii*, *Lacerta vivipara, Lagopus lagopus, Remiz pendulinus, Lepus timidus, Alces alces, Rangifer tarandus, Capreolus capreolus,* and *Canis lupus.*

（陈建伟摄）

狍
Capreolus capreolus (Credit: Chen Jianwei)

（陈建伟摄）

驯鹿
Rangifer tarandus (Credit: Chen Jianwei)

2. 华北区
2. North China Region

　　华北区北临蒙新区与东北区，南抵秦岭、淮河，西起西倾山，东临黄海和渤海。属于本区特有或主要分布于本区的华北型种类很少，只有无蹼壁虎、山噪鹛、麝鼹、林猬等。动物区系主要由东北型的广布种类所组成。蒙新区成分如小短趾百灵、凤头百灵和达乌尔黄鼠等几乎渗透贯穿全区。华北区是南、北方动物相互混杂的地带。

It is adjacent to the Inner Mongolia-Xinjiang Region and the Northeast Region in the north, Qinling Mountains and Huai River in the south, Xiqing Mountain in the west, and Yellow Sea and Bohai Sea in the east. There are few North China species specific to the region or mainly distributed in it, including only *Gekko swinhonis*, *Garrulax davidi*, *Scaptochirus moschata*, and *Hemiechinus hughi*. The fauna is mainly composed of widely distributed Northeast Chinese species. Constituents of the Inner Mongolia-Xinjiang region such as *Calandrella rufescens*, *Galerida cristata*, and the *Spermophilus dauricus* almost penetrate through the region. The North China region is intermixed by animals from the south and the north.

3. 蒙新区
3. Inner Mongolia-Xinjiang Region

　　蒙新区包括内蒙古高原和鄂尔多斯高原、阿拉善（包括河西走廊）、塔里木、柴达木和准噶尔等盆地以及天山山地等。两栖类有绿蟾蜍、花背蟾蜍、大蟾蜍。爬行类中以沙蜥、麻蜥等属的种类为最多。鸟类中的典型种类有大鸨、毛腿沙鸡和几种百灵。野骆驼、蒙古野驴、黄羊、鹅喉羚等为本区有蹄类的代表。

蒙古野驴 （陈建伟摄）
Equus hemionus (Credit: Chen Jianwei)

It includes the Inner Mongolia Plateau and the Ordos Plateau, Alashan (including the Hexi Corridor), Tarim, Qaidam and Jungar basins, as well as the Tianshan Mountains. Amphibians include *Bufo viridis*, *Bufo raddei*, and *Bufo gargarizans*. Reptiles mainly include *Lacerta agilis* and *Eremias* species. Typical species of birds include *Otis tarda*, *Syrrhaptes paradoxus*, and some larks. *Camelus ferus*, *Equus hemionus*, *Procapra gutturosa*, and *Gazella subgutturosa* are representatives of ungulates in this region.

野骆驼 （陈建伟摄）
Camelus ferus (Credit: Chen Jianwei)

鹅喉羚 （陈建伟摄）
Gazella subgutturosa (Credit: Chen Jianwei)

4. 青藏区
4. Qinghai-Tibet Region

青藏区包括青海、西藏和四川西部。动物区系主要由高地型成分组成。最典型的代表有野牦牛、藏羚和西藏野驴、藏雪鸡、黑颈鹤和多种雪雀以及温泉蛇、西藏沙蜥和青海沙蜥等。

It includes Qinghai, Tibet and western Sichuan. The fauna mainly consists of upland-type components. The most typical representatives include *Bos mutus*, *Pantholops hodgsonii*, *Equus kiang*, *Tetraogallus tibetanus*, *Grus nigricollis*, several varieties of *Montifringilla ruficollis*, *Thermophis baileyi*, *Phrynocephalus theobaldi*, and *Phrynocephalus vlangalii*.

（陈建伟摄）

藏羚
Pantholops hodgsonii (Credit: Chen Jianwei)

（陈建伟摄）

西藏野驴
Equus kiang (Credit: Chen Jianwei)

（陈建伟摄）

野牦牛
Bos mutus (Credit: Chen Jianwei)

（陈建伟摄）

黑颈鹤
Grus nigricollis (Credit: Chen Jianwei)

（二）东洋界
（Ⅱ）Oriental Realm

1. 西南区
1. Southwest Region

西南区包括四川省西部、昌都地区东部，北起青海、甘肃南缘，南抵云南南部（即横断山脉部分），向西包括喜马拉雅山脉南坡针叶林带以下的山地。动物区系的主要成分属于横断山脉—喜马拉雅分布型的种类。典型代表有兽类中的小熊猫和鸟类中的血雉和虹雉。

（陈建伟摄）

血雉
Ithaginis cruentus (Credit: Chen Jianwei)

It includes western Sichuan and east Changdu region, staring from the southern edge of Qinghai and Gansu in the north, southern Yunnan (i.e. the Hengduan Mountains) in the south, and mountainous land under the coniferous forest zone on the southern slope of the Himalayas in the west. The main components of fauna belong to the species distributed in the Hengduan Mountains – the Himalayas. The typical representatives include *Ailurus fulgens* in mammals and *Ithaginis cruentus* and several *Lophophorus* in birds.

2. 华中区
2. Central China Region

华中区包括四川盆地以东的长江流域。属于本区特有的种类很少。区内分布比较广泛的种类有东方蝾螈、隆肛蛙、灰胸竹鸡、黑麂、小麂和毛冠鹿等。

It includes the Yangtze River to the east of Sichuan Basin. There are few endemic species in this region. Species that are widely distributed in the region include *Cynops orientalis*, *Rana quadranus*, *Bambusicola thoracica*, *Muntiacus crinifrons*, *Muntiacus reevesi*, and *Elaphodus cephalophus*.

3. 华南区
3. South China Region

华南区包括云南与两广的南部，福建东南沿海一带及台湾、海南岛和南海诸岛。典型热带种有鸟类中的红头咬鹃、橙腹叶鹎和兽类中的棕果蝠等。此外，还有一些在区内广泛分布的种，如台北蛙、变色树蜥、中国壁虎、鹧鸪、白鹇、竹啄木鸟和红颊獴、花白竹鼠、青毛巨鼠等。

（陈建伟摄）

白鹇
Lophura nycthemera (Credit: Chen Jianwei)

It includes Yunnan and the south of Guangdong and Guangxi, the southeast coast of Fujian, and Taiwan, Hainan Island and the South China Sea islands. The typical tropical species include *Harpactes erythrocephalus* and *Chloropsis hardwickii* in birds and *Rousettus leschenaulti* in mammals. In addition, some species are widely distributed in the region, such as *Hylarana taipehensis*, *Calotes versicolor*, *Gekko chinensis*, *Francolinus pintadeanus*, *Lophura nycthemera*, *Gecinulus grantia*, *Herpestes javanicus*, *Rhizomys pruinosus*, and *Beryimys bowersi*.

研究性学习
Investigative Study

请同学们任意选取一个区，说明该区的动物分类特征与地理环境的关系。

Please pick any district to describe the relationship between classification and characteristics of the animals and the geographical environment in it.

拓展阅读
Extended Reading

野生动物的栖息环境
Habitats of Wildlife

我国的生态系统主要包括森林、草原、荒漠、农田、湿地及海洋六大类型。其中，森林是最重要的陆地生态系统，蕴藏了大量的生物物种，是生物多样性最为丰富的生态系统类型。我国的森林类型繁多、功能齐备，对中国乃至全球的环境和气候都具有特别重要的影响。我国的森林按气候带分布从北向南有寒温带针叶林、温带针阔叶混交林、暖温带落叶林和针叶林、亚热带常绿阔叶林和针叶林、热带季雨林、雨林。其中，亚热带森林在物种多样性及重要性方面是世界同一地带其他地区无与伦比的。中国的天然湿地包括沼泽、泥炭地、湿草甸、浅水湖泊、高原咸水湖泊、盐沼和海岸滩涂等类型，涵盖了全球 39 个湿地类型，而且青藏高原的高寒湿地在世界上为我国所独有。我国的天然湿地总面积为 2600 多万公顷（不包括河流），其中内陆和海岸湿地生态系统的面积堪称亚洲之最，除了作为许多濒危特有野生动植物的栖息地之外，它们还是迁徙鸟类，包括许多全球性受威胁物种的重要停歇地和繁殖地。

The ecosystems in China mainly include forests, grasslands, deserts, farmlands, wetlands and oceans. Among them, forests are the most important terrestrial ecosystem that bears a great number of biological species and that is the most biodiverse ecosystem types. The forests in China have many types and a wide range of functions, having a particularly significant impact on the environment and climate of China and even the world. Distributed along climatic zones from north to south, the forests in China include cold temperate coniferous forest, temperate coniferous and broad-leaved mixed forest, warm temperate deciduous and coniferous forest, subtropical evergreen broad-leaved and coniferous forest, tropical monsoon forest, and rainforest. Among them, the subtropical forest is unparalleled by other regions in the same zone of the world in terms of species diversity and importance. China's natural wetlands include marshes, peat land, wet meadows, shallow lakes, plateaus saltwater lakes, salt marshes, and coastal tidal-flat areas, covering 39 types of wetlands in the world, what's more, the alpine wetland on the Tibetan Plateau is unique in the world. The total area of natural wetlands cover over 26 million hectares (excluding rivers), of which the areas of inland and coastal wetland ecosystems rank the first in Asia. In addition to being the habitats of many endangered endemic wildlife, they are also important stopover and breeding sites of migratory birds, including many threatened species in the globe.

世界兽类之最
Top Mammals in the World

1. 蓝鲸——地球上最大的兽类
1. *Balaenoptera musculus* — The Largest Mammal on Earth

蓝鲸属哺乳纲鲸目须鲸科，是最大的鲸类，是地球上最大的哺乳动物，也是地球上现存最大的动物。体长一般为 22～33 米，体重为 150～180 吨，也就是说，它的体重相当于 25 只以上的非洲象，或者 2000～3000 个人的重量的总和。所幸的是，由于

蓝鲸
Balaenoptera musculus

海洋浮力的作用，它不需要像陆生动物那样费力地支撑自己的体重，另外庞大的身躯还有助于保持恒定的体温。1864 年，挪威人斯文德·福因用专门设计捕捉大型鲸鱼的鱼叉装配了他的轮船，这种方法很快流行起来，从此以后人类开始大量捕杀蓝鲸。由于人类的捕杀，蓝鲸的数量曾经锐减，几乎灭绝。为了防止鲸类被滥杀，1931 年，世界上第一个《国际捕鲸公约》签署。1946 年，《国际管制捕鲸公约》签订。1948 年，国际捕鲸委员会（IWC）成立，加入国际捕鲸委员会的会员国必须承认《国际管制捕鲸公约》。国际捕鲸委员会是《国际管制捕鲸公约》的执行机构，现有 61 个会员国，中国也是会员之一。从 20 世纪 60 年代起，国际捕鲸委员会开始禁止捕杀蓝鲸，此时已有 350000 头蓝鲸被杀。目前，世界上的蓝鲸可能有数万头。国际捕鲸委员会 1986 年通过了《全球禁止捕鲸公约》，严格禁止商业捕鲸。但是，依然有个别国家打着"科研"的幌子，进行捕鲸活动，加剧了鲸类的濒危，受到国际社会的谴责。

The *Balaenoptera musculus* belongs to the family Balaenopteridae of the order Cetacean of the class Mammalia. It is the largest whale species, the largest mammal, and the largest existing animal on Earth. Its body length is usually 22–33 m, weight of 150–180 tons. In other words, its weight is equal to the sum of more than 25 African elephants or the sum of 2,000–3,000 persons. Fortunately, due to the buoyancy of the ocean, it does not need to support its own weight as painfully as terrestrial animals, and its huge body also helps to maintain a constant body temperature. In 1864, a Norwegian named Svend Foyn used fish spear designed to capture large whales to assemble his ship. This approach quickly became popular, and ever since that humans began to catch and kill *Balaenoptera musculus* in large numbers. Due to the hunting of humans, *Balaenoptera musculus* population dropped drastically and the animal was almost extinct. In 1931, in order to prevent the killing of whales, the world's first *International Convention for Whaling* was signed. In 1946, the *International Convention on the Regulation of Whaling* was signed. In 1948, the International Whaling Commission (IWC) was established, and the member states of this organization must acknowledge the *International Convention on the Regulation of Whaling*. IWC is the executing agency of the *International Convention on the Regulation of Whaling*. It now has 61 member states, including China. Since the 1960s, IWC has banned the hunting of *Balaenoptera musculus*, but by then 350,000 *Balaenoptera musculus* had been killed. Currently, there may be tens of thousands of *Balaenoptera musculus* in the world. In 1986, IWC passed the *Convention on the Global Ban on Whaling* to strictly ban commercial whaling. However, some countries continued whaling under the disguise of "scientific research", which exacerbated endangered whales, and were condemned by the international community.

蓝鲸曾分布于从南极到北极之间的南北两半球各大海洋中，尤以接近南极附近的海洋中数量较多，但热带水域较为少见。我国是蓝鲸的次要分布区，在历史上，在渤海、黄海、东海、台湾海域和南海可能有分布。如果人类停止对蓝鲸的捕杀，善待蓝鲸，也许有一天在我国海域也能见到蓝鲸。

The *Balaenoptera musculus* was once distributed in the oceans of northern and southern hemispheres from the Antarctic to the Arctic, especially in the oceans close to the Antarctica, but relatively rare in tropical waters. China is the secondary distribution area of *Balaenoptera musculus*. In history, this animal might be distributed in the Bohai Sea, Yellow Sea, East China Sea, Taiwan and South China Sea. If humans stop hunting *Balaenoptera musculus* and treat them friendly, maybe they will be seen in the waters of China.

2. 象——陆地上最大的哺乳类动物
2. Elephant —The Largest Land Mammal

象属于哺乳纲长鼻目象科，是目前地球陆地上最大的哺乳类动物。多产于非洲和亚洲热带地区。象可分为非洲象和亚洲象，也有学者认为应将非洲象分为非洲草原象和非洲森林象两个种。非洲草原象的体型最大，其成年雄性的肩高可达3～4米，体

亚洲象
Elaphas maximus (Credit: Chen Jianwei)

（陈建伟摄）

重最大者可达 13 吨。

Elephants belong to the family Elephantidae of the order Proboscidea of the class Mammalia and are now the largest land mammal on Earth. They are mostly reproduced in the tropical regions of Africa and Asia. They can be classified into two types, *Loxodonta* and *Elephas maximus*. Some scholars believe that *Loxodonta* can be divided into *Loxodonta africana* and *Loxodonta cyclotis*. *Loxodonta africana* is larger in size. The shoulder height of an adult male can reach 3 – 4 m, and the largest weight can be up to 13 tons.

我国云南省南部的西双版纳、普洱和临沧等少数几个地区目前有亚洲象分布，数量仅 200～250 头，极度珍稀、濒危。由于分布区土地利用日益加剧，亚洲象栖息地岛屿化、破碎化现象严重，它们被分隔残存于几个生态孤岛上，种群间的交流受到严重阻碍，生存受到严重威胁。随着我国政府对亚洲象保护力度的不断加大，亚洲象的生存形势有望好转。

Now in China, *Elaphas maximus* is distributed in a few areas such as Xishuangbanna, Pu'er, and Lincang in southern Yunnan, and only 200 to 250 are left. They are extremely rare and endangered. Due to the increasing land use in these distribution areas, the habitats of *Elaphas maximus* are becoming more and more insular and fragmented. Since they are separated in a few ecological islands, the exchanges between populations have been severely hampered and the survival is seriously threatened. As the Chinese government is making enhanced efforts to protect *Elaphas maximus*, their survival condition is expected to be improved.

3. 虎——世界上最大的猫科动物

3. Tiger — The Largest Cat in the World

虎属于哺乳纲食肉目猫科，是目前世界上体型最大的猫科动物。东北虎是各个虎亚种中体型最大者，成年雄性东北虎体重可达 180～306 千克。虎原有 9 个亚种，遍布亚洲地区。20 世纪初全球大约有虎 10 万只，到 20 世纪 70 年代，只剩下 4000 只左右。巴厘虎、里海虎和爪哇虎相继灭绝，仅存的东北虎、华南虎、印度支那虎、马来亚虎、孟加拉虎和苏门答腊虎目前只剩下不到 3500 只，零星分布在 14 个国家。

The tiger belongs to the family Felidae of the order Carnivora of the class Mammalia and is now the world's largest cat. *Panthera tigris altaica* has the largest size among all subspecies. The weight of an adult male *Panthera tigris altaica* can be up to 180–306 kg. The tiger originally consisted of nine subspecies, distributed throughout Asia. At the beginning of 20th century, there were about 100,000 tigers in the world; by the 1970s, only about 4,000 had been left. *Panthera tigris balica*, *Panthera tigris virgata*, and *Panthera tigris sondaica* have become extinct, and only *Panthera tigris altaica*, *Panthera tigris amoyensis*, *Panthera tigris corbetti*, *Panthera tigris jacksoni*, *Panthera tigris tigris*, and *Panthera tigris sumatrae* survive, but they are fewer than 3,500 and scattered in 14 countries.

（陈建伟摄）
东北虎
Panthera tigris altaica (Credit: Chen Jianwei)

　　我国拥有的虎亚种最多，现有东北虎、华南虎、印度支那虎和孟加拉虎 4 个亚种，现存野生虎种群只有 50～60 只。2010 年，国家林业局制定了《中国野生虎恢复计划》，并由时任总理温家宝于 2010 年 11 月 23 日在俄罗斯圣彼得堡"保护老虎国际论坛"政府首脑会议上亲自宣布实施。该计划的目标是力争到中国下一个农历虎年（即 2022 年），促使我国野生虎数量大幅度增长，栖息地范围大幅度扩展。

China has the most tigris subspecies, now including *Panthera tigris altaica*, *Panthera tigris amoyensis*, *Panthera tigris corbetti*, and *Panthera tigris tigris*. The existing wild tiger population includes 50 to 60 tigers. In 2010, the State Forestry Administration developed the *China Tiger Recovery Program*, and then the Premier Wen Jiabao announced its implementation at the meeting of government heads of International Tiger Conservation Forum in St. Petersburg, Russia, on November 23, 2010. The program was aimed to drive a substantial increase of the number of wild tigers and great extension of their habitats in low range by the next year of the tiger according to Chinese lunar calendar (in 2022).

（陈建伟摄）
印度支那虎
Panthera tigris corbetti (Credit: Chen Jianwei)

（陈建伟摄）
孟加拉虎
Panthera tigris tigris (Credit: Chen Jianwei)

第二节 多姿多彩的野生动物世界
Section Ⅱ   Colorful Wildlife World

野生动物的分类有广义和狭义之分。广义上的野生动物分为兽类、鸟类、爬行类、两栖类、鱼类，以及软体动物和昆虫等。狭义上的野生动物是指除了鱼类和无脊椎动物以外的上述各类动物，即包括兽类、鸟类、爬行类和两栖类。

Wildlife can be classified in the broad and the narrow sense. In the broad sense, wildlife can be classified into beasts, birds, reptiles, amphibians, fish, mollusks and insects. In the narrow sense, wildlife refers to the above animals except fish and invertebrates, namely including beasts, birds, reptiles and amphibians.

你知道吗？
Do you know?

目前，动物分类学家根据动物的各种特征（形态、细胞、遗传、生理、生化、生态和地球分布）进行分类，即自然分类法，将动物依次分为各种等级，即界、门、纲、目、科、属、种7个主要等级。其中，种是分类所用的基本单位。每一种动物，都可以给它们在这个等级序列中冠以适当的名称和位置。例如大熊猫（拉丁学名为 *Ailuropoda melanoleuca*），属于动物界，脊索动物门、哺乳纲、食肉目、大熊猫科、大熊猫属。

Currently, animal taxonomists classify animals by various characteristics (morphology, cell, heredity, physiology, biochemistry, ecology and distribution on Earth), namely natural classification. The animals are classified into seven different levels, including kingdom, phylum, class, order, family, genus and species. Among them, species is the basic unit of classification. Every kind of animal can be named and positioned appropriately in this sequence. For example, the giant panda (whose Latin name is Ailuropoda melanoleuca), belongs to the genus Ailuropoda, the family Ailuropodidaor, the order Carnivora, the class Mammalia, the phylum Chordata, and the kingdom Animalia.

一、兽类
I. Beasts

　　兽类属于脊索动物中的哺乳纲，是由爬行类进化而来的。主要特征表现在：①体内有一条由许多脊椎骨连接而成的脊柱；②身体表面被毛；③胎生（鸭嘴兽、针鼹除外）哺乳类动物；④恒温；⑤脑颅扩大，大脑相当发达；⑥心脏左右两室完全分开；⑦牙齿分为门齿、犬齿和颊齿。

Beasts belong to the class Mammalia under the phylum Chordata and evolved from reptiles. Their main features include: ① The body has a spine connected together by a number of vertebrae; ② The body surface has hair; ③ They are viviparous (except for the platypus and the echidna) mammals; ④ They have constant temperatures; ⑤ They have expanded skulls and well-developed brains; ⑥ Their ventriculus sinisters and ventriculus dexters are completely separate; ⑦ Their teeth are divided into incisors, canine teeth and cheek teeth.

（一）我国兽类种类繁多
（ I ）Great Varieties of Beasts in China

　　有资料显示，世界现存的兽类共有 5515 种。我国有兽类 673 种（蒋志刚，2016）。我国拥有的兽类种数占世界兽类种数的 12.2%，其中许多珍稀动物为我国特有或我国是其主要分布地域。

Data show that now there are 5,515 species of beasts in the world. In China,there are 673 species of beasts (Jiang Zhigang, 2016). The varieties of beasts in China account for 12.2% of the world, and many of the rare animals are endemic to China or mainly distributed here.

（二）我国有代表性的珍稀兽类
（ II ）Representative Rare Beasts in China

（陈建伟摄）
川金丝猴
Rhinopithecus roxellana
(Credit: Chen Jianwei)

　　我国特有的重要珍稀兽类有：大熊猫、川金丝猴、滇金丝猴、黔金丝猴、海南黑冠长臂猿、台湾猴、藏酋猴、白鱀豚（又名白鳍豚）、黑麂、贡山麂、野牦牛、藏羚、普氏原羚、海南坡鹿、白唇鹿、麋鹿等。主要分布于我国的重要珍稀兽类有：小熊猫、林麝、马麝、喜马拉雅麝、獐、毛冠鹿、梅花鹿、蒙古野驴、西藏野驴、普氏野马、黑长臂猿、中国穿山甲、羚牛等。

The endemic rare beasts in China include: *Ailuropoda*

melanoleuca, *Rhinopithecus roxellana*, *Rhinopithecus bieti*, *Rhinopithecus brelichi*, *Nomascus hainanus*, *Macaca cyclopis*, *Macaca thibetana*, *Lipotes vexillifer*, *Muntiacus crinifrons*, *Muntiacus gongshanensis*, *Bos mutus*, *Pantholops hodgsonii*, *Procapra przewalskii*, *Cervus eldii*, *Cervus albirostris*, and *Elaphurus davidianus*. The rare beasts mainly distributed in China include: *Ailurus fulgens*, *Moschus berezovskii*, *Moschus chrysogaster sifanicus*, *Moschus leucogaster*, *Hydropot*, *Elaphodus cephalophus*, *Cervus nippon*, *Equus hemionus hemionus*, *Equus kiang*, *Equus ferus* ssp. *przewalskii*, *Hylobates concolor*, *Manis pentadactyla*, and *Budorcas taxicolor*.

（陈建伟摄）

普氏原羚
Procapra przewalskii (Credit: Chen Jianwei)

（陈建伟摄）

梅花鹿
Cervus nippon (Credit: Chen Jianwei)

（陈建伟摄）

滇金丝猴
Rhinopithecus bieti (Credit: Chen Jianwei)

（陈建伟摄）

中国穿山甲
Manis pentadactyla (Credit: Chen Jianwei)

（陈建伟摄）

普氏野马
Equus ferus ssp. *przewalskii*
(Credit: Chen Jianwei)

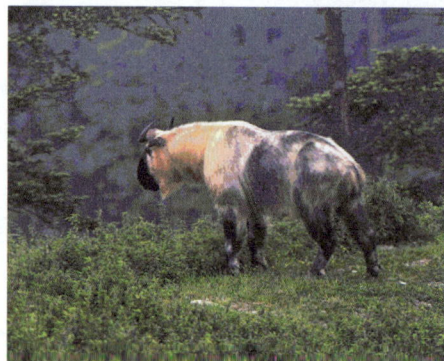

（陈建伟摄）

羚牛
Budorcas taxicolor (Credit: Chen Jianwei)

二、鸟类
Ⅱ. Birds

鸟纲是脊索动物门脊椎动物亚门的一纲。体均被羽，恒温，卵生，胚胎外有羊膜。前肢特化成翼，有时退化。多营飞翔生活。心脏是 2 心房 2 心室。骨多空隙，内充气体。呼吸器官除肺外，有辅助呼吸的气囊。

Aves belongs to the subphylum Vertebrata of the phylum Chordata. Their bodies are covered by feathers, with constant temperatures, oviparous, and with amnion outside the embryos. Their forelimbs have evolved into wings, with occasional degradation. They generally can fly. They have two atria and two ventricles. Their bones have many spaces and are filled with air. In addition to lung, their respiratory organs have air sacs to assist breathing.

鸟类是大自然的精灵。百灵的鸣唱、孔雀的开屏、天鹅的优雅、雄鹰的英姿无时无刻不给人以美感。鸟类在天际的自由翱翔更引人遐思。

Birds are fairies in nature. The singing of larks, the unfolded tails of peacocks, the elegance of swans, and the heroic posture of eagles represent a sense of beauty all the time. Those birds fly freely in the sky arouse inspiration of reveries.

（一）我国鸟类多种多样
（Ⅰ）Great Varieties of Birds in China

世界上现存的鸟类共有 10426 种，其中在我国发现、记录到的鸟类有 1372 种。我国鸟类约占世界鸟类种数的 13.2%，是世界上鸟类分布种数最多的国家之一。

Now there are over 10,426 species of birds in the world. There are 1,372 species of birds in China. The varieties of birds in China account for about 13.2% of the world, and China is one of the countries with the most varieties of birds in the world.

（二）我国有代表性的珍稀鸟类
（Ⅱ）Representative Rare Birds in China

我国是"雉类王国"，其中比较知名的雉类有褐马鸡、黄腹角雉、绿尾虹雉、红腹锦鸡、白冠长尾雉、台湾的蓝鹇等。世界上鹤科鸟类共有 15 种，见于我国的就有 9 种，如丹顶鹤、白鹤、黑颈鹤、灰鹤、蓑羽鹤等。我国的雁鸭类有鸿雁、豆雁、斑头雁、大天鹅、小天鹅、疣鼻天鹅、中华秋沙鸭、鸳鸯等。朱鹮是稀世珍禽，我国民间把朱鹮看作吉祥的象征，称为"吉祥之鸟"。历史上朱鹮曾广泛分布于东亚地区，包括中国东部、日本、俄罗斯、朝鲜等地。20 世纪中叶以来，由于人类社会生产活动对环境的影响，朱鹮的数量急剧下降，分布区域急剧缩小。目前，野生朱鹮种群仅在我国有分布。

China is "a kingdom of pheasants". The more well-known pheasants here include *Crossoptilon mantchuricum, Tragopan caboti, Lophophorus lhuysii, Chrysolophus pictus, Syrmaticus reevesii*, and *Lophura swinhoii* from Taiwan. There are 15 birds in the family Gruidae in the world, 9 of which are found in China, including *Grus japonensis, Grus leucogeranus, Grus nigricollis, Grus grus*, and *Anthropoides virgo*. The anatidae varieties in China include *Anser cygnoides, Anser fabalis, Anser indicus, Cygnus cygnus, Cygnus columbianus, Cygnus olor, Mergus squamatus*, and *Aix gadericulata*. *Nipponia nippon* is a rare bird and is called an "auspicious bird" as symbol of good luck according to Chinese folklore. In history, *Nipponia nippon* was widely distributed in the East Asia, including eastern China, Japan, Russia, and North Korea. Since the mid 20th century, due to the impact of production activities of human society on the environment, there have been sharp declines in the number and distribution areas of *Nipponia nippon*. At present, the bird is distributed only in China.

（陈建伟摄）

褐马鸡
Crossoptilon mantchuricum
(Credit: Chen Jianwei)

（陈建伟摄）

丹顶鹤
Grus japonensis (Credit: Chen Jianwei)

（陈建伟摄）

灰鹤
Grus grus (Credit: Chen Jianwei)

（陈建伟摄）

蓑羽鹤
Anthropoides virgo (Credit: Chen Jianwei)

（陈建伟摄）

朱鹮
Nipponia nippon (Credit: Chen Jianwei)

（陈建伟摄）

大天鹅
Cygnus cygnus (Credit: Chen Jianwei)

（陈建伟摄）

小天鹅
Cygnus columbianus (Credit: Chen Jianwei)

（陈建伟摄）

疣鼻天鹅
Cygnus olor (Credit: Chen Jianwei)

三、爬行类、两栖类及其他野生动物
III. Reptiles, Amphibians and Other Wildlife

爬行类动物属于脊椎动物亚门。它们的身体构造和生理机能比两栖类更能适应陆地生活环境。两栖类动物也属于脊椎动物亚门，由鱼类进化而来。长期的物种进化使两栖动物既能活跃在陆地上，又能游动于水中；与动物界中其他种类相比，地球上现存的两栖动物的物种较少，目前正式被确认的种类约有 4000 种。除了兽类、鸟类、爬行类和两栖类动物以外，我国还有一些其他动物类群。

Reptiles belong to the subphylum vertebrata. Their body structures and physiological functions allow them to be more adaptive to the terrestrial living environment than amphibians. Amphibians also belong to the vertebrata. They evolved from fish. Long-term evolution has allowed amphibians to be both active in the land and swim in the water; compared with other varieties in the animal kingdom, there are few species of amphibians now existing on the Earth. Now about 4,000 species are officially confirmed. In addition to beasts, birds, reptiles and amphibians, there are some other animal species in China.

（一）我国爬行类、两栖类动物多样性
（Ⅰ）Diversity of Reptiles and Amphibians in China

我国爬行类、两栖类动物种类繁多、丰富多样。

The reptiles and amphibians in China are various and diverse.

扬子鳄是我国国家一级保护野生动物，是世界上仅有的两种淡水鳄之一，另一种是美国密西西比鳄（又名：美国短吻鳄）。成年的扬子鳄可以长到 2 米，那么它是不是地球上最小的鳄呢？不是的，世界上最小的鳄是非洲的侏鳄，体长 1.8 米，但扬子鳄是世界上最小的短吻鳄。

Alligator sinensis is a national level protected species in China, and is one of the only two freshwater crocodile species in the world. The other is *Alligator mississippiensis*. Given that an adult Chinese alligator can grow up to 2 m at most, can we say it is the smallest crocodile on the Earth? No, the smallest crocodile in the world is the *Osteolaemus tetraspis*, whose body length is 1.8 m. But *Alligator sinensis* is the smallest species in the family Alligatoridae in the world.

（陈建伟摄）

扬子鳄
Alligator sinensis (Credit: Chen Jianwei)

侏鳄
Osteolaemus tetraspis

据初步统计，世界上现存的两栖类共有 7493 种，我国有 408 种。我国现有两栖类种数约占世界总数的 5.4%。世界上现存的爬行类共有 10272 种，我国有 461 种。我国现有爬行类种数约占世界总数的 4.5%。

According to preliminary statistics, now there are 7,493 species amphibians in the world. There are nearly 408 species in China. The varieties of amphibians in China account for 5.4% of the world. Now there are 10,272 species of reptiles in the world. There are nearly 461 species in China. The varieties of reptiles in China account for 4.5% of the world.

两栖类中的大鲵（娃娃鱼）为我国国家二级保护野生动物，是世界上最大的两栖类动物，一般身长 60～70 厘米，最大可达 1 米，体重 5～6 千克。爬行类中的鳄蜥科为我国特有，仅有 1 属 1 种，即中国鳄蜥。

The amphibian *Andrias davidianus* are the grade Ⅱ protected species in China and the world's largest amphibian. Generally its body length is 60 –70 cm, with the maximum up to 1 m, and its weight is about 5–6 kg. The family Shinisauridae in reptiles is endemic to China, with only one species of one genus, i.e. *Shinisaurus crocodilurus*.

（陈建伟摄）

大鲵
Andrias davidianus (Credit: Chen Jianwei)

中国鳄蜥
Shinisaurus crocodilurus

（二）我国的其他珍稀野生动物
（Ⅱ）Other Rare Wildlife in China

除了鸟类、兽类、两栖类和爬行类中的一些种类外，其他动物类群中的宽吻鱼（新疆大头鱼）、中华鲟、达氏鲟、白鲟、红珊瑚、库氏砗磲、鹦鹉螺、中华蛩蠊、金斑喙凤蝶、多鳃孔舌形虫、黄岛长吻虫也是我国特别珍稀的野生动物。

新疆大头鱼
Aspiorhynchus laticeps

In addition to some species of birds, beasts, amphibians and reptiles, there are some rare species of other types in China, including *Aspiorhynchus laticepts, Acipenser sinensis, Acipenser dabryanus, Psephuyrus gladius, Corallium rubrum, Tridacna gigas, Nautilus, Galloisiana sinensis, Teinopalpus aureus, Glossobalanus polybranchioporus,* and *Saccoglossus hwangtauensis.*

中华鲟
Acipenser sinensis

金斑喙凤蝶
Teinopalpus aureus

研究性学习
Investigative Study

　　请观看"人与自然"节目，谈一谈地球上最凶猛的野生动物有哪些？并为我们介绍一下它们的体貌特征与生活习性。

Please watch the program "Human and Nature" and name some of the most ferocious wildlife on the planet. And introduce their physical characteristics and living habits.

拓展阅读
Extended Reading

动物与文化
Animal and Culture

一、兽类与文化
I. Beasts and Culture

（一）我国的虎文化
（Ⅰ）Tiger Culture in China

　　我国的虎文化源远流长，与龙文化互为纽带，贯穿于整个中华文化。在文学、雕塑、绘画、戏曲，以及民间传说、神话故事和儿歌中，崇虎敬虎的思想无处不在，降虎伏虎的事迹时常出现。远古时代有虎图腾崇拜，民间有穿戴虎头鞋帽和张贴老虎年画的习俗。

The tiger culture in China has a long history and ties with the dragon culture to run throughout the Chinese culture. In literature, sculpture, painting, drama, and folklore, fairy tales and nursery rhymes, worship of tiger is found everywhere and stories of conquering tigers often occurred. In ancient times, there was tiger totem worship, and people had the custom of wearing shoes and hats with tiger patterns and putting up New Year pictures of tiger.

武松打虎
Wu Song fights the tiger

老虎年画
new year picture of tiger

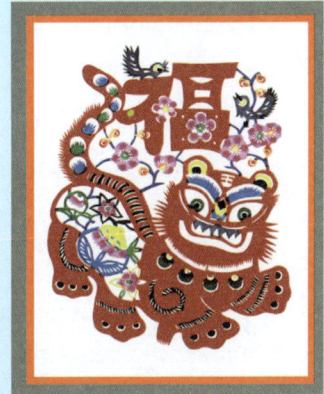

　　汉语中有虎啸生风、虎背熊腰、生龙活虎、虎踞龙盘、龙腾虎跃、如虎添翼、虎视眈眈、龙争虎斗、龙潭虎穴、降龙伏虎、虎口拔牙、不入虎穴焉得虎子等许多成语。春秋战国及以后许多朝代都使用过调兵遣将的虎符；人们常用虎将、虎师、虎威、虎步等词语描述英勇善战的军队或军人。

古代青铜虎符
ancient bronze tiger tally

In the Chinese language, there are many phrases associated with tiger, such as "vigorous like tigers", "strong as a bear in the hips and with a back supple as a tiger's", "doughty as a dragon and lively as a tiger", "like a coiling dragon and crouching tiger", "dragons rising and tigers leaping (which describes a scene of bustling activity)", "might redoubled like a tiger with wings", "looking at fiercely as a tiger does", "a gigantic struggle between two equally-matched forces like a dragon and a tiger", "a dragon's pond and a tiger's cave to describe dangerous places", "subdue the dragon and tame the tiger (overcome powerful adversaries)", "pull a tooth from the tiger's mouth (dare to confront the greatest danger)", and "How can one obtain tiger-cubs without entering the tiger's lair? (Nothing ventured, nothing gain.)" During the Period of Spring and Autumn Warring States and many dynasties, tiger-shaped tallies were used by

generals for troop movement; people use "Tiger General", "Tiger Division", "prowess of a general like a tiger", and "a great warrior's firm strides like the tiger's" to describe the heroic army or soldiers.

（二）其他国家兽类与文化的联系
（Ⅱ）Association between Beasts and Culture in Other Countries

1. 青龙白虎之邦——韩国
1. A State of Dragon and Tiger — South Korea

韩国文化中很多方面与虎有关，源于韩国人对虎的信仰。韩国民间称虎为"山神爷"，认为虎是正义的化身，对虎特别喜爱、尊重。韩国人称东北虎为韩国虎（高丽虎）。1950 年，东北虎从韩国土地上消失。虽然野生的虎已灭绝，但韩国人仍称自己的国度为"青龙白虎之邦"。

Many aspects of Korean culture are tiger-associated and these originated from the Korean belief in tiger. Korean folk called the tiger as "God of Mountains". Believing that tiger is the embodiment of justice, they show particular love and respect for the tiger. The South Koreans call *Panthera tigris altaica* the South Korean tiger (or the Korean Tiger). In 1950, *Panthera tigris altaica* disappeared from South Korea. Although wild tigers have become extinct, the Koreans still call their country as "a state of dragon and tiger".

2. 一些国家国徽上的兽类
2. Beasts in National Emblems of Some Countries

印度国徽
national emblem of India

印度国徽图案来源于孔雀王朝阿育王石柱顶端的石刻。圆形台基上站立着三只金色的狮子，象征信心、勇气和力量。台基四周有四个守卫四方的守兽：东方是象、南方是马、西方是牛、北方是狮。

The national emblem of India is originated from the stone inscription on the top of the Ashoka Pillar in Maurya Empire. Three golden lions stand on the circular foundation, symbolizing confidence, courage and strength. Four beasts guard on the foundation in the four directions: elephant in the east, horse in the south, bull in the west, and lion in the north.

芬兰国徽上挺立的金狮头戴王冠，披着护甲的右前肢挥舞着一把银色宝剑，象征着要驱逐一切来犯之敌；金狮脚踩一把弯刀，表示对来自东方的敌人的蔑视；9朵白玫瑰花点缀在金狮周围，分别代表组成芬兰的9个省。

The golden lion on the national emblem of Finland wears a crown, is dressed in the armor, and holds a silver sword with its right forelimb to symbolize that it will expel every invading enemy; the golden lion stands on a machete, which indicates contempt of the enemies from the East; the nine white roses dotted around the golden lion represent the nine provinces of Finland.

芬兰国徽
national emblem of
Finland

澳大利亚国徽
national emblem of
Australia

澳大利亚国徽上的红色狮子象征塔斯马尼亚州，国徽上面的袋鼠和鸸鹋（也被称为澳洲鸵鸟）是澳大利亚的象征。

The red lion on the national emblem of Australia symbolizes Tasmania, and the kangaroo and *Dromaius novaehollandiae* (also known as Australian ostrich) are symbols of Australia.

加拿大国徽
national emblem of
Canada

加拿大国徽上有五只金色的狮子和一只红色的狮子及一只独角兽。独角兽是西方国家传说中的动物，形如白马，额前有一个螺旋角，代表高贵、高傲和纯洁。英国国徽上有狮子和独角兽的图案。缅甸国徽上也有狮子图案。

There are five golden lions, one red lion and a unicorn on the national emblem of Canada. Unicorn in western countries is a legendary animal, shaped like a white horse, with a helix angle on the forehead, symbolizing nobleness, pride and purity. There are lion and unicorn pattern on the national emblem of the UK. The national emblem of Burma also has the lion pattern.

马来西亚国徽两侧各站着一头虎，两虎后肢踩着金色饰带，饰带上书写着格言"团结就是力量"。

Two tigers stand on both sides of the national emblem of Malaysia. The hind legs of the two tigers step on golden ribbons, which are inscribed with the motto "Unity is strength".

马来西亚国徽
national emblem of
Malaysia

柬埔寨国徽左右两侧各由有一头大象和狮子，守护着共有五层的华盖。

The both sides of the national emblem of Cambodia have an elephant and a lion to guard the five-storey canopy.

柬埔寨国徽
national emblem of
Cambodia

二、鸟类与文化

Ⅱ. Birds and Culture

鸟类在世界各国都与文化息息相关。例如，丹顶鹤在我国自古以来就被人们称为仙鹤，古典小说《西游记》中所述神仙太白金星的坐骑便是丹顶鹤。世界上许多国家的国徽上都绘有鸟类图案。澳大利亚国徽上就有黑天鹅、鸸鹋图案。1960年，在日本东京召开的第12届国际鸟类保护会议的与会代表，呼吁世界各国都选出本国的国鸟，以在国民中普及保护鸟类的思想。据统计，世界上已有120多个国家和地区确定了国鸟和区鸟。目前我国还没有确定国鸟。我国曾有野生动物保护组织建议将红腹锦鸡（俗名金鸡）、丹顶鹤、朱鹮、天鹅、褐马鸡、相思鸟、猎隼、喜鹊、黑脸琵鹭、绿孔雀等作为国鸟的候选者，其中呼声较高的是红腹锦鸡和丹顶鹤。

Birds are closely linked with culture all over the world. For example, *Grus japonensis* in China has been called "holy crane" since ancient times. The ride of the God named Great White Planet in the classic novel *Journey to the West* was *Grus japonensis*. The national emblems of many countries in the world are painted with bird patterns. The national emblem of Australia has the patterns of *Cygnus atratus* and *Dromaius novaehollandiae*. In 1960, the delegates at the 12th International Conference on the Protection of Birds convened in Tokyo, Japan, called on the world countries to elect their own national bird and popularize the thought of bird protection among citizens. According to statistics, more than 120 countries and regions in the world have determined their national bird or regional bird. At present, China has not yet determined its national bird. Wildlife conservation organizations have recommended candidates like *Chrysolophus pictus* (commonly known as golden pheasant), *Grus japonensis, Nipponia nippon, Cygnus, Crossoptilon mantchuricum, Leiothrix lutea, Falco cherrug, Pica pica, Platalea minor*, and *Pavo muticus*. Among them, *Chrysolophus pictus* and *Grus japonensis* were most strongly recommended.

清代一品文官补服
embroidery on the uniform of highest-rank civil official in Qing Dynasty

（一）我国的鸟类文化

（Ⅰ）Bird Culture in China

在我国，千百年来，丹顶鹤的形象都是"吉祥、长寿、幸福、安康、忠贞"的象征。丹顶鹤在我国古代也被称为"仙鹤"，象征着"品性高洁"。清代一品文官补服（即官服胸口部分的一块刺绣品）上即绣有丹顶鹤图案。在我国的国画和刺绣中经常能看到松树和丹顶鹤在一起的图案，寓意为"高洁、长寿"。实际上，丹顶鹤是水禽，将丹顶鹤和松树画在一起只是人们的美好想象。

In China, for thousands of years, *Grus japonensis* has been symbols of "good luck, longevity, happiness, well-being, and loyalty". *Grus japonensis* was also known as "holy crane" in ancient China and symbolized "noble character."The embroidery on the uniform of the highest-rank civil official in Qing Dynasty (i.e. the part on the chest of the official uniform) was adorned with a pattern of *Grus japonensis*. In Chinese paintings and embroidery, patterns of pine and *Grus japonensis* are often seen for the implication of "nobleness and longevity". In fact, *Grus japonensis* is a waterfowl, and to combine *Grus japonensis* with pine on paintings is just wonderful imagination of people.

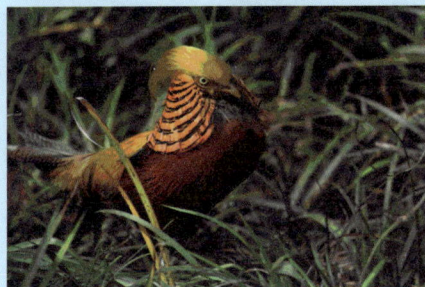

（陈建伟摄）
红腹锦鸡
Chrysolophus pictus (Credit: Chen Jianwei)

　　另外，我国民间有"金鸡报喜"一说，金鸡指的就是我国特有鸟类红腹锦鸡。孔雀、鸳鸯也被我国人民认为是吉祥鸟类。

In addition, there is a folk saying in China that "Golden pheasant can report good news". Golden pheasant is the *Chrysolophus pictus* endemic to China. *Peafowl* and *Aix galericulata* are also considered as auspicious birds by Chinese people.

　　（二）其他国家的鸟类文化

　　（Ⅱ）Bird Culture in Other Countries

　　1. 俄罗斯国徽上的双头鹰

　　1. Double-headed Eagle on the National Emblem of Russia

　　1993 年 11 月 30 日，俄罗斯联邦共和国决定采用以双头鹰为图案的国徽：红色盾面上有一只金色的双头鹰，鹰头上是三顶王冠，鹰爪抓着权杖和金球。双头鹰雄视东西两边，代表俄罗斯是一个地跨欧亚两大洲的国家；三顶王冠象征着国家是统一的俄罗斯联邦；金球和权杖象征国家的统一是神圣不可侵犯的。

俄罗斯国徽
national emblem of Russia

On November 30, 1993, the Federal Republic of Russia decided to adopt the national emblem with a pattern of double-headed eagle on it: there is a golden double-headed eagle on the red shield, with the head of the eagle wearing three crowns and the claw holding a truncheon and a golden ball. The double-headed eagle is looking ferociously at the east and west directions, meaning that Russia is a large country across the European and the Asian continents; the three crowns symbolize the unified Russian Federation; the golden ball and the truncheon symbolize that national unity is sacred and inviolable.

2. 美国国鸟——白头海雕
2. National Bird of the U.S. — *Haliaeetus leucocephalus*

白头海雕
Haliaeetus leucocephalus

美国是世界上最先确定国鸟的国家。在美国独立之后不久的 1782 年 6 月 20 日，美国总统克拉克和美国国会通过决议立法，选定白头海雕为美国国鸟，视其为"力量、勇气、自由和不朽"的象征。白头海雕（又名美洲雕）是大型猛禽，成年时体长可达 1 米，翼展 2 米多长。白头海雕仅分布在北美沿海，是北美洲的特产物种，体态威武雄健，深受美国人民的喜爱。今天，无论是美国的国徽，还是美国军队的军服上，都描绘着一只白头海雕，它一只脚抓着橄榄枝，另一只脚抓着箭，象征着和平与强大武力。白头海雕作为美国国鸟受到了法律保护，1982 年里根总统宣布每年的 6 月 20 日为白头海雕日。

The United States was the first country in the world to determine a national bird. On June 20, 1782, shortly after the independence of the United States, President Clark and the U.S. Congress passed a resolution on the legislation of selecting *Haliaeetus leucocephalus* as the national bird of the United States, as it was considered as the symbol of "strength, courage, freedom and immortality". The *Haliaeetus leucocephalus* is a large bird of prey. The body length of an adult *Haliaeetus leucocephalus* can be up to 1 m and the wingspan can reach 2 m. *Haliaeetus leucocephalus* are distributed only along the coast of North America and are endemic species in North America. It has a powerful and robust posture and is loved by the American people. Today, both the national emblem of the United States and the uniform of United States Army are adorned with a *Haliaeetus leucocephalus*: The bird clutches an olive branch with one foot and an arrow with the other foot, symbolizing peace and powerful force. As the national bird of the United States, *Haliaeetus leucocephalus* is subject to legal protection. In 1982, President Reagan declared June 20 as the Bald Eagle Day every year.

3. 德国国鸟——白鹳
3. National Bird of Germany —*Ciconia ciconia*

白鹳
Ciconia ciconia

在欧洲，自古以来白鹳就一直被认为是"带来幸福的鸟"，是吉祥的象征，是上帝派来的"天使"，是专门来拜访交好运的人的。老人们也常对小孩子说，"婴孩都是鹳鸟送来"，所以人们又称它为"送婴鸟"。

在德国，自白鹳被选为国鸟以后，不少家庭特地在烟囱上筑造了平台，供它们筑巢用。
In Europe, *Ciconia ciconia* has been considered as "a bird that brings happiness", a symbol of good luck, an "angel" sent by God, and a bird that visits fortunate people only since ancient times. Old people often told children, "Children are sent by storks". So people also call it "child sending bird". In Germany, after *Ciconia ciconia* was selected as the national bird, many households specially built a platform on their chimneys for them to nest with.

4. 英国国鸟——红胸鸲
4. National Bird of the UK — *Erithacus rubecula*

红胸鸲，又名知更鸟，是英国人最熟悉、最喜欢的一种小鸟。红胸鸲在繁殖期间，鸣声特别悦耳动听。1960 年英国国民投票将其选定为国鸟。
Erithacus rubecula, also known as the robin, is the most familiar and favorite small bird in the UK. During breeding, the bird sings particularly melodious songs. In 1960, the British nationals voted to select it as the national bird.

红胸鸲
Erithacus rubecula

5. 新西兰国鸟——几维鸟
5. National Bird of New Zealand — *Apteryx*

几维鸟，是无翼鸟科 3 种鸟类（褐几维、大斑几维、小斑几维）的共同名称。几维鸟的平均大小与人们常见的大公鸡差不多，褐几维鸟和大斑几维鸟体形稍大，小斑几维鸟较小。几维鸟是新西兰的特产，也是新西兰的国鸟及象征。新西兰的两角与一元的钱币上面印有几维鸟的图像。

几维鸟
Apteryx

Apteryx refers to any of a small genus of 3 flightless New Zealand birds (namely *Apteryx australis*, *Apteryx haastii*, and *Apteryx owenii*) in the family Apterygidae. The average size of a *Apteryx* is similar to that of a rooster commonly seen, while *Apteryx australis* and *Apteryx haastii* are slightly larger and *Apteryx owenii* is slightly smaller. The *Apteryx* is endemic to New Zealand and is the national bird and symbol of New Zealand. The coins of twenty cents and one dollar in New Zealand are minted with the pattern of a *Apteryx*.

新西兰的两角与一元的钱币
the twenty-cent and one-dollar coins of
New Zealand

6. 印度国鸟——蓝孔雀

6. National Bird of India —*Pavo cristatus*

　　在印度神话传说中，天神迦尔迪盖耶骑着蓝孔雀云游四方，耆那教神祖的交通工具也是蓝孔雀，印度教大神因陀罗封蓝孔雀为鸟王。1963 年 1 月，印度政府宣布蓝孔雀为国鸟。

In Indian myths and legends, the God Shanmukha rode a *Pavo cristatus* to travel, and the vehicle of ancestral god of Jainism was also a *Pavo cristatus*. The bird was honored by Indra, the Hindu god, as the King of Birds. In January 1963, the Indian government announced *Pavo cristatus* as the national bird.

蓝孔雀
Pavo cristatus

7. 特立尼达和多巴哥国鸟——蜂鸟

7. National Bird of Trinidad and Tobago —*Trochilidae*

　　特立尼达和多巴哥国徽上半部是黑色背景中左右对称的两只蜂鸟，这是特立尼达和多巴哥的国鸟，被人们视为给万物带来生机的"太阳神"，也是美丽祖国的象征。蜂鸟象征人民不畏强权、酷爱独立和自由的精神。

The upper half of the national emblem of Trinidad and Tobago is two symmetrical *Trochilidae* against a black background. *Trochilidae* is the national bird of Trinidad and Tobago and is considered as "Titan" that brings life to creatures and symbol of the beautiful motherland. It symbolizes the spirit of no fear of hegemony and the passion for independence and freedom.

蜂鸟
Trochilidae

第二章 野生动物生存危机
Chapter Ⅱ Survival Crisis of Wildlife

近几百年来，在人类对野生动物的过度利用、生境丧失、生境破碎化、生境退化与污染、全球气候变化、外来物种入侵、重大灾害、疾病等因素的影响下，造成了野生动物濒临灭绝的后果，给野生动物的生存带来了重重危机。本章将了解造成野生动物生存危机的因素及保护野生动物资源的重要意义。

In recent centuries, the impact of human overuse of wildlife, habitat loss, habitat fragmentation, habitat degradation and pollution, climate change, invasion of alien species, major disasters, and diseases has led to endangered wildlife and a survival crisis. In this chapter, we will look at the factors that have contributed to that survival crisis for wildlife as well as the importance of protecting wildlife resources.

第一节 野生动物濒危原因
Section Ⅰ Causes for Endangerment of Wildlife

你知道吗？
Do you know?

生境破碎化是指大片、连续的生境不仅面积减小，而且被分割为两个或更多的片断。

Habitat fragmentation refers to not only a decrease in the total area of the habitat but its division into two or more pieces.

一、人类对野生动物的过度利用
I. Human Overuse of Wildlife

1. 工业革命之前的移民与利用造成部分物种灭绝
1. Migration and Utilization before the Industrial Revolution Led to the Extinction of Some Animals

人类出现的历史伴随着人类利用野生动植物的历史。野生动物曾经是人类蛋白质的主要来源。从人类移民到澳洲、南北美洲初始，人类开始对生物灭绝速度具有显著影响。在土著居民于大约 6 万年前从亚洲来到澳大利亚之后，90% 的大型有袋类动物已经绝种。15000~12000 年前，印第安人的祖先经白令海峡到达美洲，之后美洲大陆的猛犸、剑齿虎等数十种大型哺乳动物和鸟类开始绝种。大约 1000 年前，毛利人从波利尼西亚迁移至新西兰，仅用了 500 年的时间就使得数百万计身型巨大的恐鸟灭绝。

The history of mankind was accompanied by the history of human use of wildlife. Wildlife was once a major source of protein for man. Since humans began to migrate to Australia and to North and South Americas, they have had a significant impact on the rate of biological extinction. Since the indigenous population arrived in Australia from Asia about 60,000 years ago, 90% of large marsupials have gone extinct. The ancestors of the Indians arrived in America by way of the Bering Strait 15,000–12,000 years ago, and after that dozens of large mammals and birds, including *Mammuthus* and *Machairodus*, began to go extinct. About 1,000 years ago, the Maoris migrated from Polynesia to New Zealand and it took them only 500 years to make *Dinornithidae*, which numbered millions in its heyday, go extinct.

猛犸
Mammuthus

剑齿虎
Machairodus

恐鸟
Dinornithidae

2. 工业革命之后人口增加，对自然资源的过度开发和利用

2. The Population Grew after the Industrial Revolution and the Natural Resources were Excessively Exploited and Utilized

人类对野生动物多样性的影响在近几百年来显著加剧。尤其在工业革命（大约始于 1750 年）之后，世界上的人口呈爆炸性指数式增长。1850 年世界人口为 12 亿，到 2000 年世界人口已达 60 亿。更多的人口意味着需要更多的自然资源，从而造成了对自然资源的过度开发和利用。20 世纪以来，随着捕鲸船吨位的增加，鲸类被人类一种

接一种地摧毁。据 1993 年统计，与捕鲸业开展前相比，蓝鲸（地球上目前最大的动物）减少 94%，露脊鲸减少 74%，座头鲸减少 92%。有资料表明，在过去的 300 年里至少有 21 种海洋物种在全球范围内灭绝，位于食物链顶端的肉食性鱼类中 90% 已经在海洋里消失。

座头鲸
Megaptera novaeangliae

Human impact on wildlife diversity has increased significantly in recent centuries. Especially during the Industrial Revolution (beginning around 1750), the population of the world exploded exponentially. In 1850, the world population reached 1.2 billion, and in 2000 it climbed to 6 billion. More population means a greater need for natural resources, resulting in the overuse and over-utilization of natural resources. Since the 20th century, with the increase in the tonnage of whalers, different species of whales have been destroyed by humans successively. According to the 1993 statistics, compared with the numbers before whaling began in earnest, *Balaenoptera musculus*, (now the largest animal on the Earth) had decreased in population by 94%, *Eubalaena japonica* by 74%, and *Megaptera novaeangliae* 92%. Data show that at least 21 marine species have become extinct worldwide over the past 300 years and 90% of carnivorous fish at the top of the food chain has disappeared from the oceans.

二、生境丧失与生境破碎化
II. Habitat Loss and Fragmentation

1. 生境丧失
1. Habitat Loss

　　人口的增长导致对土地的需求不断增加，大面积的森林、草地和湿地变成了城镇、村庄、道路、农田和牧场，野生动物的生境正逐步被人类占领而渐趋丧失。

Population growth leads to increased demand for land, and large areas of forests, grasslands and wetlands were turned into towns, villages, roads, farmland, and pastures. The habitats of wildlife are being occupied by humans and lost gradually.

某机场削平 65 座山头建成，造成野生动物生境丧失
an airport built by removing 65 mountain tops, leading to habitat loss of wildlife

2. 生境破碎化
2. Habitat Fragmentation

生境碎片
habitat fragments

野生动物生境丧失的同时，几乎总是伴随着生境的破碎化。野生动物的生境曾经占据着广大、完整的土地，而如今已被公路、农田、乡村和其他大范围的人类建筑分割成生境片断，这就是生境破碎化过程。

The loss of habitats for wildlife is almost always accompanied by habitat fragmentation. Wildlife habitats each used to usually occupy a single vast piece of land, but now they have been divided by roads, farmland, villages, and other large buildings into habitat fragments, which is the process of habitat fragmentation.

三、生境退化与污染
III. Habitat Degradation and Pollution

即使野生动物的生境没有受到明显的破坏或破碎化的影响，野生动物所处的生态系统也可能会受到人类活动带来的深远影响。生境退化最普遍的形式是遭受污染，污染常常是由杀虫剂、污水、农用化肥、工业化合物与废弃物、工厂与机动车排放气体等因素导致。环境污染有时是清晰可见的、影响显著的；但有些污染是隐蔽的、不可见的，却可能带来巨大的危害。

Even if the wildlife habitats were not significantly damaged or fragmented, the ecosystems in which wildlife lives would likely be subject to the far-reaching impact of human activities. The most common form of habitat degradation is pollution, which is often caused by pesticides, sewage, agricultural fertilizers, industrial compounds and waste, emissions from factories and motor vehicles, etc. Environmental pollution is sometimes visible and has significant impact; but some pollution can be hidden and invisible but may bring great harm.

海洋溢油造成生境污染
habitat pollution caused by ocean oil spill

长江边的排污，造成中华鲟生境破坏
pollution discharge in the Yangtze River leads to damage to *Acipenser sinensis* habitats

四、全球气候变化
Ⅳ. Climate Change

自工业革命以来，尤其是近百年来，人类对煤炭、石油、天然气的利用不断增加，人类的工业生产、生活导致排放到大气中的二氧化碳、甲烷、氧化亚氮等气体含量一直稳步增加，这些气体像温室的玻璃一样，可以透射太阳光，并将由太阳能转化的热能存留于温室内，因此使地球温度升高，这种效应被称作温室效应。由于引起温室效应气体的增加，全球气候出现变化，最近100年来，全球气候变暖。全球气候变化对生物

全球气候变暖造成动物生存危机
global warming posing a survival crisis to wild animals

多样性的影响是多方面的，不同类型的生态系统受到的威胁程度有所差别。全球气候变化将使北温带和南温带气候区向极地偏移，有学者估计会有超过 10% 的动植物种不能生存于变暖的气候中。

Since the Industrial Revolution, especially over the past century, human use of coal, oil, and natural gas has been constantly on the rise, and so have the emissions of carbon dioxide, methane, and nitrous oxide into the atmosphere caused by human industrial production and human life. These greenhouse gases, like the glass used in greenhouses, can transmit sunlight and retain the heat converted from solar energy in the greenhouse, thus leading to a rise in the temperature of the Earth. This effect is called the greenhouse effect. Due to the increase in greenhouse gases, the global climate begins to change. Global warming has been going on over the past 100 years. The impact of climate change on biodiversity is varied, and the degrees of threat to different types of ecosystems are different. Climate change will make the northern and southern temperate zones shift toward the Polar Regions. Some scholars have estimated that more than 10% of plant and animal species will not survive in warmer climate.

五、外来物种入侵
V. Invasion of Alien Species

1. 外来物种入侵对本地物种的影响
1. Impact of Alien Species Invasion on Native Species

外来物种是指由于人类有意或无意引入，在远离其原产地以外地区生存的物种。大多数外来物种由于不适应新环境而无法在新生境中存活。然而，有些外来物种却能在新生境中建立种群，成为入侵种。入侵种可以通过竞争有限资源替代本地种，也可

传播松材线虫的松墨天牛
Monochamus alternatus that spreads
Bursaphelenchus xylophilus

能直接捕食本地种使之濒临灭绝，或者通过改变生境使本地种不能继续生存。有学者认为，外来物种入侵已经成为物种濒危与灭绝的第二大因素，仅次于生物生存自然环境的改变。在美国，威胁濒危物种生存的各类因素中，外来物种入侵占威胁因素的49%，特别是对鸟类和植物带来了严重影响。

Alien species refers to those that live in areas far from their origins due to intentional or unintentional human introduction. Most alien species cannot survive in a new habitat because of their inability to adapt to the new environment. However, some alien species are able to establish populations in new habitats and become invasive species. Invasive species can replace native species by competing for limited resources and they may also directly prey on native species and endanger them or prevent them from surviving by changing their habitats. Some scholars believe that the invasion of alien species has become the second major factor behind the endangerment and extinction of species, only next to the change of survival and natural environment of creatures. In the United States, among many factors that threaten the survival of endangered species, the invasion of alien species accounts for 49%, posing a serious threat to birds and plants particularly.

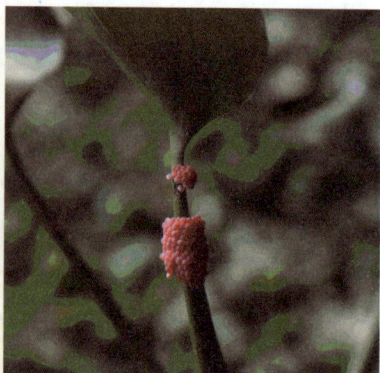

（陈建伟摄）
外来物种——福寿螺的卵
alien species —eggs of the *Pomacea canaliculata* (Credit: Chen Jianwei)

（陈建伟摄）
崇明东滩的外来物种入侵——互花米草逐渐占据了本地芦苇的地盘
invasion by alien species of Chongming Dongtan —*Spartina alterniflora* gradually occupying the habitat of native reed (Credit: Chen Jianwei)

2. 谨慎 "放生"

2. Be Careful with "Freeing Captive Animals"

在我国，出于"行善"目的的不合理"放生"可能会给自然生态系统带来巨大的生态风险。如巴西龟是世界公认的"生态杀手"，已被我国列入外来入侵物种，禁止"放生"野外。巴西龟又称红耳龟或称巴西翠龟，其原产地并非位于巴西，而是在北美密西西比河及格兰德河流域，现已被不少家庭当作宠物来养殖或观赏。巴西龟被世界自然保护联盟列为 100 种最危险的入侵者之一，其活动能力强、食性杂，繁殖速度快，进入天然水体之后，会侵占大量生存资源，占据本地龟类和鱼类的生存空间。

(陈建伟摄)

外来物种——红耳龟
alien species — *Trachemys scripta elegans*
(Credit: Chen Jianwei)

In China, the improper "freeing of captive animals" for the purpose of "doing good" may result in huge ecological risks to the natural ecosystems. For example, *Trachemys scripta elegans* is recognized worldwide as an "ecological killer" and has been listed as an invasive alien species in China. It is prohibited to "release" it in the wild. *Trachemys scripta elegans*, originated not in Brazil but in the drainage basins of the Mississippi River and the Rio Grande in North America. It now has been kept in many families as pets or for ornamental purposes. *Trachemys scripta elegans* is listed by the International Union for Conservation of Nature as one of the 100 most dangerous invaders. Characterized by its strong activity, miscellaneous eating habit, and fast reproduction, it will occupy a lot of resources for survival and encroach on the living space of native turtles and fish upon entering a natural body of water.

研究性学习
Investigative Study

同学们，你或者家人有过"放生"的经历吗？请查阅资料说明不能随意放生的野生动物有哪些，正确的处理办法是什么？

Did you or your family have the experience of "releasing captive animals"? Please consult some materials and explain which wildlife cannot be released casually and what correct measures can be taken to deal with them.

拓展阅读
Extended Reading

保护野生动物就是保护人类自己
Protecting Wildlife is Protecting Humans Themselves

——历史给我们的启示
— A Lesson from History

在 20 世纪 60 年代以前，几乎找不到"环境保护"这个词。那时流行于世界许多地方的口号是"向大自然宣战""征服大自然"。当时，由于人类科学技术的大幅进步和跨越式发展、生产力水平大大提高，在许多国家，大自然成了人们征服与控制的对象，而非保护并与之和谐相处的对象。然而人类对自然的践踏和破坏很快就使自己受到了惩罚。

Before the 1960s, the phrase "environmental protection" was seldom heard. What was popular in many parts of the world back then was "declaring war on nature" and "conquering nature". At the time, due to significant advances in science and technology and resultant leaps in development and productivity, nature became the object of human conquest and control rather than something to be protected or live in harmony with. However, humans' abuse and destruction of nature soon made themselves punished.

1. 农药 DDT 的危害
1. Harm of DDT

农药 DDT 及其毒性的发现者、瑞士化学家保罗·赫尔满·米勒获 1948 年诺贝尔生理学或医学奖。应用 DDT 这类杀虫剂，杀灭了蚊子和其他的害虫，使农作物提高了产量，同时也杀灭了益虫。更可怕的是，在接受过 DDT 喷撒后，许多种昆虫能迅速繁殖抗 DDT 的种群。由于 DDT 会积累于昆虫的体内，这些昆虫成为其他动物的食物后，那些动物，尤其是鱼类、鸟类，则会中毒而被危害。由于食物链的传导等原因，甚至在没有使用 DDT 的南极地区，在企鹅体内也发现有 DDT 存在。所以，喷洒 DDT 只是获得近期的利益，却牺牲了长远的利益。

Paul Hermann Müller, the Swiss chemist who discovered the pesticide DDT and its toxicity, won the 1948 Nobel Prize in Physiology or Medicine. However, the application of pesticides like DDT also kills beneficial insects while killing mosquitoes and other pests to improve crop yields. It was even more frightening that, many insects could quickly multiply populations that resist DDT after being sprayed with DDT. Because DDT can accumulate in the bodies of insects, animals that eat these insects, especially fish and birds, will be poisoned. Because of the transmission of poisons by food chain and other reasons, DDT was even found in the bodies of penguins in the Antarctic although DDT was not used there. Thus, spraying DDT only got short-term benefits at the expense of the long-term ones.

2. "橙剂"的使用及危害
2. Use and Harm of "Agent Orange"

1967—1971 年，为防止越南游击队袭击，美军开始使用化学落叶剂 —— 一种高效的除草剂，因其容器的标志条纹为橙色，故名"橙剂"。美军用飞机向越南丛林中喷洒了 7600 万升落叶型除草剂，清除了遮天蔽日的林木树叶。美军喷洒"橙剂"的面积占越南南方总面积的 10%，其中 34% 的地区不止一次被喷洒。越战后，"橙剂后遗症"逐渐显现，越南人民和参加越战的美国老兵深受其害。"橙剂"中含有毒性很强的化学物质"二噁英"，其化学性质十分稳定，很难自然降解消除。它还能通过食物链在自然界循环，贻害范围非常广泛。

From 1967 to 1971, in order to prevent the attack of Vietnamese guerrilla, the U.S. military began using a chemical defoliant — a highly effective herbicide that was named "Agent Orange" because of the orange stripes on its container. The U.S. military sprayed 76 million liters of the substance on the jungles of Vietnam to clear the sheltering tree leaves. The area that received the spray of "Agent Orange" from the U.S. military accounted for 10% of the total area in South Vietnam, with 34% of the sprayed area receiving more than one spray. After the Vietnam War, the "after effects of Agent Orange" gradually emerged, and both the Vietnamese people and the U.S. veterans who fought in the war suffered greatly. "Agent Orange" contains a highly toxic chemical substance named "dioxin", which has a very stable chemical nature and is difficult to eliminate through natural degradation. It can also cycle through the food chain in nature, leaving a wide range of harm.

受"橙剂"危害的人，其身体出现了各种病变。更为严重的是，毒素改变了他们的生育能力和遗传基因。在越南长山地区，人们经常会发现一些缺胳膊少腿或浑身溃烂的畸形儿，还有很多白痴儿童。这些人就是"橙剂"的直接受害者。此外，在南方服役过的军人妻子的流产率也非常高。美国的越战老兵们也深受"橙剂"之苦。目前除糖尿病外，美国越战老兵所患的病中，已有 9 种疾病被证实与"橙剂"有直接关系，包括心脏病、前列腺癌以及各种神经系统疾病等。

People who were harmed by "Agent Orange" suffered a variety of diseases. More seriously, the toxin changed their fertility and genetics. In the Truong son Ra areas of Vietnam, people often find deformed children with missing arms or legs or festering all over the body and many mentally retarded children. They are the direct victims of "Agent Orange". In addition, the wives of soldiers who ever served in the south suffered a higher abortion rate. The American veterans who fought in the Vietnamese War also suffered from "Agent Orange". Now, in addition to diabetes, 9 diseases that these America veterans suffer have been confirmed to be directly related to "Agent Orange", including heart disease, prostate cancer, and a variety of neurological diseases.

3.《寂静的春天》开启全球环境保护的里程碑
3. *Silent Spring* Marks the Milestone in Worldwide Environmental Protection

曾在美国鱼类及野生动植物管理局工作过的美国海洋生物学家蕾切尔·卡逊敏锐地看到了人类不尊重大自然肆意妄为的恶果。1962 年，蕾切尔·卡逊出版了著名的环境保护读物《寂静的春天》，这是一本引发了全世界环境保护事业的书，书中描述了人类可能将面临一个没有鸟、蜜蜂和蝴蝶的世界。这本书提示我们，人类对农药的使用要适度。正是这本不寻常的书，在世界范围内引起人们对野生动物的关注，唤起了人们的环境意识，这本书同时引发了公众对环境问题的注意，促使环境保护问题提到了各国政府面前，各种环境保护组织纷纷成立，从而促使联合国于 1972 年 6 月 12 日在斯德哥尔摩召开了"人类环境大会"，并由各国签署了"人类环境宣言"，开启了自然、环境和野生动物保护事业。

Rachel Carson, an American marine biologist who once served in the United States Fish and Wildlife Service, was among the earliest observers to see the consequences of reckless illegal human behavior that disrespected nature. In 1962, Rachel Carson published a famous book on environmental protection titled *Silent Spring*. Helping to set the global environmental protection movement in motion, the book describes a world without birds, bees or

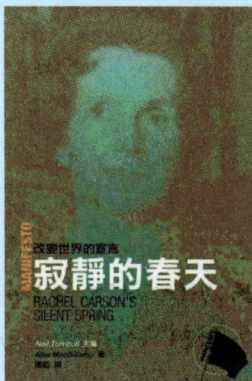

《寂静的春天》
Silent Spring

世界环境日会标
the logo of the World Environment Day

butterflies that humans might face. It reminds us that humans should use pesticides moderately. It is this unusual book that caused worldwide concern for wildlife and heightened people's environmental awareness. It also drew public attention to the environmental issues and raised them before governments. Various environmental groups were established, thereby pushing the United Nations to hold the "United Nations Conference on the Human Environment" in Stockholm on June 12, 1972, and sign a declaration in the process. The conference marked the protection of nature, the environment, and the wildlife as a cause to be furthered by everybody.

第二节　保护野生动物的意义
Section Ⅱ　Importance of Protecting Wildlife

近一二百年来，全球物种灭绝速度急剧上升，人类对野生动物的灭绝越来越负有不可推卸的责任。对野生动物的保护已迫在眉睫。野生动物是大自然的宝贵财富，野生动物具有多方面的重要价值，保护野生动物，对维护生物多样性及生态安全、推动生态文明和美丽中国建设具有重要意义。

Over the past one or two centuries, the extinction rate of global species rose sharply. Humans are increasingly responsible for the extinction of wildlife. The protection of wildlife is imminent. Wildlife is a valuable asset of nature and its valuableness is reflected in many respects. Protecting wildlife has important implications for the conservation of biodiversity and ecological security and the construction of ecological civilization and a beautiful China.

你知道吗？
Do you know?

第四纪更新世时期是一个地质学名词，是第四纪的第一个世，距今约260万年至1万年。更新世冰川作用活跃。亦称洪积世（从2588000年前到11700年前），地质时代第四纪的早期。显著特征为气候变冷、有冰川期与间冰期的明显交替。

The Pleistocene Epoch of the Quaternary Period is a geographical term and is an epoch in the Quaternary period, dating back to about 2.6 million years to 10,000 years ago. Glaciation was active during the epoch, which is also known as the diluvial epoch (from 2,588,000 years ago to 11,700 years ago) as an early geological time of the Quaternary Period. The significant features of this epoch included a cooling climate and obvious alternation between glacial and interglacial periods.

一、保护野生动物，防止其灭绝
I. Protect Wildlife to Prevent Extinction

1. 生物灭绝的原因
1. Causes for Biological Extinction

在遥远的地质年代，如第四纪更新世时期，冰川期和间冰期的频繁更替导致地质和气候变化剧烈，促使物种迁徙或演化，某些物种的分布和数量迅速减少甚至消失。世界上已经灭绝的动物种类数以亿计，已无法统计。仅就兽类来说，若把化石兽类一并考虑在内，我国历史上已绝灭的兽类种类不在少数。如北京房山区周口店中国猿人遗址，距今约 69 万年，处于更新世中期，在该遗址中发现了诸如三趾马、剑齿虎和梅氏犀等兽类化石。

During those distant geological times, such as the Pleistocene Epoch of the Quaternary Period, frequent alternation between the glacial and interglacial periods led to dramatic changes in geology and climate, prompting species migration or evolution. Some species decreased rapidly in distribution and abundance and even disappeared. Hundreds of millions of animals in the world became extinct and the number was impossible to calculate. For only beasts, if fossilized beasts are included, the number of extinct beast species in China was considerable in history. For example, the historic site of *Homo erectus pekinensis* in Zhoukoudian, Fangshan District, Beijing, dated back to about 690,000 years ago in the mid-Pleistocene Epoch. Fossils of beasts like the *Hipparion*, *Machairodus* and *Dicerorhi nusmerckii* were found there.

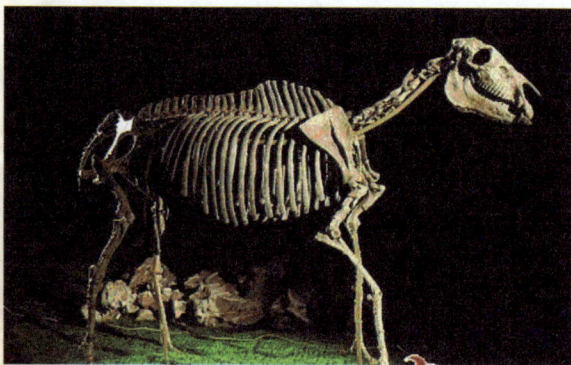

三趾马化石
fossil of *Hipparion*

梅氏犀
Dicerorhi nusmerckii

人类诞生以来，特别是人类进入文明社会以后，生物灭绝速度大大增加。许多动物，如美洲乳齿象等美洲动物的灭绝，就可能与人类进入美洲有关。人类工业化革命以来，特别是近一二百年以来，物种灭绝的速度空前提高。如北美旅鸽从几十亿只到绝种只用了几十年的时间。人类活动造成地球生态环境急剧变化是生物灭绝的主要原因。森林被大量砍伐、过度捕杀、栖息地被破坏等原因使野生动物面临越来越艰难的处境。
Since the birth of mankind, especially after the emergence of civilized society, the extinction rate of creatures has been greatly increased. The extinction of many American animals, such as *Mammut*, may have something to do with the discovery of America. Since the Industrial Revolution, especially over the past one or two centuries, the extinction rate of species has been higher than ever before. For example, it only took several decades for *Ectopistes migratorius* to become extinct from billions. Drastic changes in the global environment caused by human activities are the main reason for extinction. Due to large-scale deforestation, over-hunting, and habitat destruction, wildlife is facing an increasingly difficult situation.

美洲乳齿象
Mammut

北美旅鸽
Ectopistes migratorius

灭绝并非匀速渐进过程，而是经常在某个时间断面大规模集群发生。在集群灭绝过程中，往往是整个分类单元中的所有物种都灭绝，而且还常常是很多不同的生物类群一起灭绝，但总有其他一些类群幸免于难，还有一些类群从此诞生或开始繁盛。
Extinction is never a gradual process with a constant speed but often occurs to large-scale clusters during a particular period of time. During the process of mass extinction, generally all the species of the classified unit are extinct, and usually many different biological groups become extinct together. However, some other groups can always survive, and some groups are born or begin to flourish.

自从 6 亿年前多细胞生物在地球上诞生以来，物种大灭绝现象已经发生过 5 次。地球第一次物种大灭绝发生在距今 4.4 亿年前的奥陶纪末期，大约有 85% 的物种灭绝。在距今约 3.65 亿年前的泥盆纪后期，发生了第二次物种大灭绝，海洋生物遭到重创。

而发生在距今约 2.5 亿年前二叠纪末期的第三次物种大灭绝，是地球史上最大最严重的一次，估计地球上有 96% 的物种灭绝，其中 90% 的海洋生物和 70% 的陆地脊椎动物灭绝。第四次发生在 1.85 亿年前，80% 的爬行动物灭绝了。第五次发生在 6500 万年前的白垩纪，也是为大家所熟知的一次，统治地球达 1.6 亿年的恐龙灭绝了。这 5 次物种大灭绝事件，主要是由于地质灾难和气候变化造成的。

Since 600 million years ago, the phenomenon of mass extinctions have occurred five times after the birth of multicellular organisms on Earth. The first mass extinction on the Earth occurred about 440 million years ago, during the Late Ordovician, with the species extinction about 85 percent. In dating back about 365 million years ago, the late Devonian, the second extinction occurred, with matine organisms been hit heavily. About 250 million years ago, at the end of the Permian, the Earth occurred the third mass extinction, which is the largest and most serious one, with the extinction of 90% marine life and 70% terrestrial vertebrate. The fourth happened 185 million years ago, and 80 percent of reptiles extinct. The fifth happened 65 million years ago during the Cretaceous, the dinosaurs who once ruled the Earth 160 million years extincted, which is known to everyone. These five extinction events mainly due to the geological disaster and climate change.

2. 消失的物种
2. Disappearing Species

目前普遍认为地球生物有着超过 30 亿年的历史。古生物学家估计，地球上曾存在过 50 亿 ~500 亿种物种，而其中的 99.9% 都已灭绝。地球上现存的物种有多少种呢？海伍德（1995）认为，目前地球物种的估计值在 1000 万 ~1500 万种。

It is widely accepted that life on Earth has a history of more than 3 billion years. Paleontologists estimate that 5 to 50 billion species existed on the Earth, of which 99.9% have been extinct. How many extant species now on the Earth? Heywood believed in 1995 that now there were an estimated about 10 to 15 million species existing on the Earth.

自工业革命以来，地球上已有冰岛大海雀、北美旅鸽、南非斑驴、印尼巴厘虎、澳洲袋狼、直隶猕猴、台湾云豹等物种不复存在。有学者估计，近百年来，在人类干预下的物种灭绝比自然速度快了 1000 倍。英国科学家指出，在过去 40 年中，英国本土的鸟类种类减少了 54%，本土的野生植物种类减少了 28%，而本土蝴蝶的种类更是惊人地减少了 71%。一直被认为种类和数量众多，有很强恢复能力的昆虫也开始面临灭绝的命运。据估计，全世界目前每天有 75 个物种灭绝。学者们推断，自工业革命开始，地球就已经进入了第六次物种大灭绝时期。

Since the industrial revolution, species like *Pinguinus impennis*, *Ectopistes migratorius*,

Equus zebra, *Panthera tigtis*, *Thylacine*, *Macaque*, and *Neofelis nebulosa* have disappeared on the Earth. Some scholars estimate that over the past century, human intervention in the extinction of species is 1,000 times faster than natural rate. The British scientists pointed out that in the past 40 years, the native species of birds have been decreased 54%, local wild plant species have been decreased 28%, while the local butterfly species was strikingly reduced by 71%. The insects who have been considered as numerous types and quantities and strong ability to recover themselves have begun to face the fate of extinction. It is estimated that currently there are 75 species become extinct every day worldwide. Judging from some scholars, since the beginning of the industrial revolution, the Earth had entered the sixth mass extinction period.

正是因为人类对多数物种的灭绝负有不可推卸的责任，所以人类要正视自己的错误，采取措施防止物种灭绝。

It is because humans are inescapably responsible for the extinction of majority species that they must face up to their mistakes and take measures to prevent the extinction of species.

二、野生动物具有重要的价值
Ⅱ. Important Values of Wildlife

野生动物具有经济价值、观赏价值、文化和美学价值、科学价值和生态价值等。正因为野生动物具有巨大的价值，所以我们要保护它们，善待它们，合理地、有限度地利用它们。

Wildlife has economic, ornamental, cultural and aesthetic, scientific, and ecological value. Because wildlife has great values, we need to protect them, treat them properly, and utilize them reasonably and within limits.

1. 经济价值
1. Economic Value

对于世界上许多地方的原住民来说，捕捉野生动物是他们生活方式的组成部分，是他们的谋生之道。美国和加拿大的一些土著居民，如因纽特人，至今仍以捕捉鱼和海兽来解决衣食问题。对这些土著人来说，捕捉野生动物可能是他们唯一的生活和经济来源。

For aboriginal residents in many parts of the world, capturing wildlife is an integral part of their lifestyle and their livelihood. Some aboriginal residents in the United States and Canada, such as Inuit, still make a living by catching fish and sea animals. For these indigenous people, capturing wildlife is probably their only source of income.

2. 观赏价值
2. Ornamental Value

上海海洋水族馆
Shanghai Ocean Aquarium

我国各地的动物园、野生动物园、水族馆等，每年都要接待数以亿计的参观者。人们特别喜欢观赏野生动物，儿童更是百看不厌。观赏野生动物不仅使我们得到了快乐、增长了知识，也使我们受到了热爱自然、爱护野生动物的科普教育。

Zoos, wildlife parks, and aquariums around China receive hundreds of millions of visitors every year. People are particularly fond of appreciating wildlife, especially children, who are never tired of doing that. Appreciating wildlife not only gives us happiness and increases our knowledge, but also teaches us to love nature and care for wildlife.

3. 文化和美学价值
3. Cultural and Aesthetic Value

野生动物在人类的文化发展中，几乎无处不在。很多国家都有自己的国鸟及省（州）鸟，描写野生动物生活的书籍在世界各国都是很畅销的。相信许多同学都读过法国著名昆虫学家兼文学家法布尔的《昆虫记》。《昆虫记》的语言非常简洁优美，法布尔先生描述的每种昆虫形象栩栩如生，十分可爱，同学们甚至可以透过文字看到它们的喜怒哀乐，故事情节兼具科学性和趣味性，能够激发同学们的阅读兴趣和对大自然的神秘好奇心，培养同学们尊重生命、亲近自然、热爱科学探索的精神。

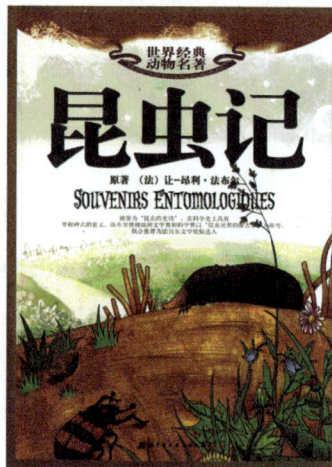

《昆虫记》
Souvenirs Entomologiques

Wildlife is almost everywhere in the development of human culture. Many countries have their own national and provincial (state) birds. Books describing lives of wildlife are popular around the world. Many students must have read *Souvenirs Entomologiques*, a book written by the famous French writer and entomologist Jean-Henri Casimir Fabre. Mr. Fabre described each insect vividly as a cute being with simple and beautiful language in *Souvenirs Entomologiques*. Students can even feel their emotions from the words. The stories are both scientific and fun to stimulate students' interest in reading and curiosity about the mysterious nature and foster their spirit to respect life, to get close to nature, and to be passionate about scientific inquiry.

4. 科学价值
4. Scientific Value

野生动物是科学研究的重要对象。现代医学、生物学、遗传学、生态学等很多领域的研究，都离不开对野生动物的研究。对古代动物化石的研究，使人们了解了动物的漫长进化过程。达尔文（1859）就是通过对世界各地野生动物、植物的观察和历史资料的综合分析，创立了进化论和自然选择学说，并发表了著名的《物种起源》。

Wildlife is an important object of scientific research. Modern medicine, biology, genetics, ecology, and research in many other fields are inseparable from the study of wildlife. Research on ancient animal fossils helps people understand the long evolutionary process of animals. Darwin (1859) created the theories of evolution and natural selection and published the famous *On the Origin of Species* through a comprehensive analysis of the wildlife and plants and historical information around the world.

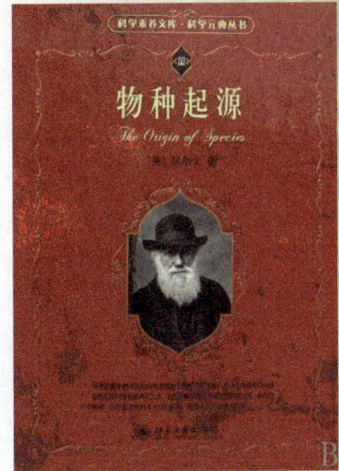

《物种起源》
On the Origin of Species

野生动物还在仿生学上给人以启迪。鸟类的体形和飞翔能力，启发了人们对飞机的研制，深海探测器等仪器模仿的是动物的蛋的原理。还有很多仿生学的实例，动物在这里发挥着不可多得的科学研究价值。

Wildlife is also inspirational in bionics. The figure and flying ability of birds inspire people to develop aircraft. Instruments like deep-sea detectors imitate the principle of animal eggs. There are many other examples of bionics in which animals turned out to be scientifically valuable.

5. 保护野生动物，维护生态平衡
5. Protecting Wildlife and Maintaining Ecological Balance

近几十年来，由于环境污染、栖息地丧失以及滥捕滥猎等原因，世界各地的许多野生动物数量正急剧减少，很多种类已濒临灭绝，生态系统的平衡遭到了破坏，给人类自身也带来了灾难。人类对狐狸、某些鼬类动物以及猛禽的过度捕猎，使森林、草原及农田中的鼠类猖獗；人类对农药的大量使用，使食虫鸟的数量大为减少，随之而来的是松毛虫和蝗虫的大发生，给农林牧业达成了巨大损失。为了维护生态平衡，必须保护野生动物。

In recent decades, due to environmental pollution, habitat loss, overfishing, and indiscriminate hunting, the number of wild animals around the world has been in drastic decline, many species are at the verge of extinction, and the balance of ecosystems is destroyed. All of this results in disasters for human beings. Excessive hunting of foxes, some weasel species, and birds of prey by humans has led to rampant murine problems in forests, grassland, and farmland; the heavy use of pesticides by humans has led to a great reduction in the number of insectivorous birds, followed by outbreaks of dendrolimus punctatus and locusts, thereby causing great losses in agriculture, forestry, and animal husbandry. In order to maintain the ecological balance, it is essential to protect wildlife.

研究性学习
Investigative Study

同学们，请读一读法布尔的《昆虫记》，写一篇读后感。
Please read Fabre's *Souvenirs Entomologiques* and write down your reflection.

拓展阅读
Extended Reading

消失的野生动物
Disappearing Wildlife

一、国外近几百年来灭绝的几种野生动物

I. Some Wild Species That Have Gone Extinct Overseas Over the Centuries

1. 渡渡鸟

1. *Raphus cucullatus*

渡渡鸟
Raphus cucullatus

渡渡鸟，又称毛里求斯渡渡鸟，是仅产于印度洋毛里求斯岛上一种不会飞又跑不快的鸟。渡渡鸟长得有些像火鸡，翅膀很小，头部很大，嘴巴是钩型的。"渡渡"在葡萄牙语的意思就是"笨笨"。人们发现这种肥硕可爱、温驯笨拙的鸟儿居然美味可口。这种鸟在被发现后不到 200 年的时间里，便由于人类的捕杀和人类活动的影响彻底灭绝。

1681 年最后 1 只渡渡鸟被人类枪杀。

Raphus cucullatus, also known as the Mauritius dodo, was a bird that was seen only on the island of Mauritius in the Indian Ocean. It could not fly and ran slowly. The bird looked somewhat like the turkey because it had small wings, a big head, and a hook-shaped mouth. The word "Dodo" means "stupid" in Portuguese. People found this stout, cute, and tame bird delicious. In less than 200 years after its discovery by humans, this bird became extinct due to hunting and other human activities. In 1681, the last *Raphus cucullatus* was shot dead by a person.

2. 斑驴
2. *Equus zebra*

斑驴曾分布于南非广袤的草原上，它们听觉灵敏，善于奔跑。在对付被称为"兽中之王"的狮子的过程中，牛羚、鸵鸟和斑驴的默契配合成为动物界的一个传奇。鸵鸟有良好的视力，牛羚有灵敏的嗅觉，而斑驴的听力异乎寻常，三者取长补短，发挥了神奇的效用。一旦出现狮子的踪影，它们相互传递信息，很快逃之夭夭。斑驴由于肉鲜美且出肉量高，因此一直是非洲人主要猎食的对象，但原始的狩猎方法并没有给斑驴群体以致命打击。直到 19 世纪，欧洲移民大量涌入非洲，他们采用套索、火器等装备进行疯狂的猎捕，还大肆劫掠、贮藏、盗运斑驴的皮张。到了 19 世纪中期，非洲南部已经很少再能见到斑驴了。世界上最后一头斑驴是饲养在荷兰的阿姆斯特丹动物园的一头雌驴，她孤苦伶仃地活到 1883 年。

小斑驴
a young *Equus zebra*

Equus zebra was once distributed in the vast grassland of South Africa. It had keen ears and was good at running. When they were confronted with the lion — the "king of beasts", the tacit cooperation among *Connochaetes*, *Struthio camelus*, and *Equus zebra* became a legend in the animal kingdom. *Struthio camelus* had good vision; *Connochaetes* had an acute sense of smell; *Equus zebra* had exceptionally keen hearing. The three complemented each other to everyone's advantage. Once a lion came into sight, they would pass information to each other and soon flee. Since there was a lot of delicious meat in its body, *Equus zebra* had been one of the major objects of hunting to Africans. However, the primitive hunting method did not give a fatal blow to *Equus zebra* as a species. Not until the 19th century did European immigrants flock to Africa in large number and use lassos, firearms and other devices to hunt the animal ruthlessly and also loot, store and illegally transport *Equus zebra* hide. By the mid 19th century, *Equus zebra* was rarely seen in southern Africa. The last *Equus zebra* in the world was a female one kept in Amsterdam Zoo, Netherlands. She lived lonely until 1883.

3. 无齿海牛

3. *Hydrodamalis gigas*

无齿海牛
Hydrodamalis gigas

无齿海牛又叫斯特拉大海牛、巨海牛，其身躯庞大，体长可达6~10米，体重5000~6400千克。无齿海牛栖息于北太平洋冷水区域的浅海地带，常常十几头或几十头组成一个群体。1741年6月，俄国人维·白令率领的探险队船只遇险，斯特拉等幸存者则漂流到了科曼多尔群岛，发现了沿海的无齿海牛。1742年，靠捕杀无齿海牛充饥得以生还的斯特拉等回到了堪察加，并带回了无齿海牛的皮和肉。此后，俄国的皮毛商人纷纷来到科曼多尔群岛。1768年无齿海牛灭绝。无齿海牛从被人类发现到灭绝只用了二十多年的时间。

Hydrodamalis gigas, also known as the giant sea cow, had a large body with a length up to 6–10 m and weighed 5,000–6,400 kg. *Hydrodamalis gigas* lived in the shallow cold waters in the North Pacific Ocean, often appearing in dozens or scores. In June 1741, the Russian Vitus Bering led an expedition vessel and ran into trouble. Stella and other survivors then drifted to the Commander Islands, discovering the animal along the coast. In 1742, having survived by killing the animal for food, Stella returned Kamchatka and brought its skin and meat with him. Since then, Russian fur traders came to the Commander Islands for the animal. In 1768, *Hydrodamalis gigas* became extinct. It took only a mere more than two decades for the species to be discovered and become extinct.

4. 比利牛斯山羊

4. *Capra pyrenaica pyrenaica*

比利牛斯山羊是一种野生山羊，又称布卡多山羊，是西班牙山羊的一个亚种。比利牛斯山羊体型大，体长1.2米左右，体重达60千克以上。它的角别具一格，像两把弯刀倒长在羊头上，威风凛凛。这个物种曾经数量众多，广泛分布在西班牙和法国的山区中。20世纪初期其数量急剧下降。最后一只自然繁殖的比利牛斯山羊死于2000年1月6日，她的名字叫作"西莉亚"。在"西莉亚"死亡前不久，科学家从它的耳部提取了皮肤细胞，保存在液氮中。在2009年，科学家利用"西莉业"的遗传物质成功克隆出一头雌性的比利牛斯山羊，这是首次已经灭绝的物种被成功复制出来。可惜的是，小山羊在出世不久就因为肺部有缺陷而夭折。

比利牛斯山羊
Capra pyrenaica pyrenaica

Capra pyrenaica pyrenaica was a wild goat, also known as Bucardo in Spanish, and was a subspecies of *Capra pyrenaica*. *Capra pyrenaica pyrenaica* had a large size, a length of about 1.2 m, and a weight of up to 60 kg or more. It had unique horns, which looked like two machetes protruding majestically from the goat's head. This species once existed in large numbers and was widely distributed in the mountainous regions of Spain and France. In the early 20th century, its number dropped sharply. The last naturally bred *Capra pyrenaica pyrenaica* died in on January 6, 2000, and her name was "Celia". Shortly before the death of "Celia", scientists had extracted skin cells from its ears and stored them in liquid nitrogen. In 2009, scientists used the genetic material of "Celia" to successfully clone a female *Capra pyrenaica pyrenaica*. That was the first extinct species to be successfully reproduced. Unfortunately, the small goat died of lung defects born shortly after its birth.

过度狩猎、偷猎、疾病以及无力与其他物种竞争食物可能是导致比利牛斯山羊灭绝的原因。

Excessive hunting, poaching, disease, and inability to compete for food with other species were probably the causes for the extinction of *Capra pyrenaica pyrenaica*.

二、我国近现代灭绝或野生灭绝的几种野生动物
Ⅱ. Some Wild Animals That Have Gone Extinct in Modern China

1. 新疆虎
1. *Panthera tigris lecoqui*

新疆虎曾主要生活在我国新疆中部塔里木河与玛纳斯河流域。在 20 世纪初，在塔里木河流域，在楼兰古城一带的绿洲，在胡杨林边，还经常有野猪、马鹿和虎出没。由于人类经济活动的增加、猎杀以及塔里木河改道等原因，新疆虎于 1916 年灭绝了。

Panthera tigris lecoqui mainly lived in the drainage basins of the Tarim River and Manasi River in central Xinjiang in China.

新疆虎
Panthera tigris lecoqui

In the early 20th century, *Sus scrofa*, *Cervus elaphus* and tigers were often seen in the oasis and desert poplar forest around the ancient city of Loulan. Due to increased human economic activities, hunting and diversion of the Tarim River, *Panthera tigris lecoqui* became extinct in 1916.

2. 麋鹿
2. *Elaphurus davidianus*

(陈建伟摄)
麋鹿
Elaphurus davidianus
(Credit: Chen Jianwei)

麋鹿是我国特产兽类，俗称"四不像"。麋鹿在数百年前主要分布在我国黄河流域及淮河流域下游的沼泽地区，最北可分布到辽宁南部。为了适应在泥泞地中行走，蹄极宽大，颇像牛蹄，又称其"蹄似牛而非牛"。 随着沼泽地被开垦成良田，无芦苇和菖蒲等高秆挺水植物可隐蔽，使麋鹿无处栖息和觅食，再加上过度猎捕，其数量日益减少。至清代，野生麋鹿已绝灭。幸而在北京南苑（南海子）清王朝御猎苑中还驯养着一群麋鹿供帝王射猎。1865 年法国传教士大卫在南苑发现了麋鹿，得到标本运回国。此后，英、法、德、比等国将麋鹿陆续运回欧洲达几十只，在各国动物园中展出。其中，英国贝福特公爵在乌邦寺别墅驯养的一群，繁殖出的个体最多，运往世界各地已达 1000 多只。然而北京南苑所驯养的麋鹿却绝灭了：1894 年北京永定河发大水，南苑洪水泛滥，跑掉一批麋鹿，被灾民捕食；1900 年八国联军侵入北京，把剩下的麋鹿全部猎杀。新中国成立后，中英建交，1956 年和 1973 年英国伦敦动物学会先后送回 4 对麋鹿，分别在北京和上海动物园内驯养。1985 年和 1986 年又赠送回来 20 只和 39 只麋鹿，分别养在北京南苑南海子和江苏大丰。目前，我国已将部分麋鹿放归自然。

Elaphurus davidianus is a beast endemic to China. Hundreds of years ago, the deer were mainly distributed in the swampy areas in the lower reaches of the Yellow River and Huai River, as north as in southern Liaoning Province. In order to walk in the mud, they have extremely wide hooves, very similar to cattle hooves. Thus, the animal was described as "having hooves very similar to those of cattle but not cattle". As marshland was reclaimed into fertile farmland, without the shelters of emergent aquatic plants with high stems, such as reeds and calamus, the deer lost their habitats and food sources. What's worse, with excessive hunting, their number was diminished. By the Qing Dynasty, the wild deer had been extinct. Fortunately, a group of domesticated deer were kept in the imperial hunting area of the Qing Dynasty in Nanyuan (Nanhaizi), Beijing, so that the emperors could have fun hunting them. In 1865, the French missionary David found the deer in Nanyuan and shipped their specimen home. After that, Britain, France, Germany, and Belgium shipped dozens of deer to Europe and exhibited them at the national zoos. Among them, the group of deer raised by the Duke of Bedford in Woburn Abbey in Britain was reproductive and more than 1,000 of their offspring were transported to other parts of the world. However, the domesticated deer raised in Nanyuan in Beijing were extinct. In 1894, a flood broke out in Yongding River in Beijing. A group of deer fled from the flood in Nanyuan and were hunted by the flood victims for food; in 1900, the Eight-power Allied Forces invaded Beijing, hunting and killing all of the remaining deer. After the founding of new China, China and Britain established diplomatic ties in 1956, and the Zoological Society of London from Britain returned four pairs of deer in 1956 and in 1973. These deer were kept at zoos in Beijing and Shanghai. In 1985 and 1986, 20 and 39 deer were returned to China and they were respectively raised in Nanhaizi of Nanyuan, Beijing, and Dafeng, Jiangsu. Now, China has released some of the deer back to the wild.

3. 普氏野马
3. *Equus ferus* ssp. *przewalskii*

我国曾生存的野马，学名叫普氏野马，也称准噶尔野马或蒙古野马。曾经广泛分布于欧亚大陆中高纬度的草原和荒漠草原地带。我国是普氏野马的原产国之一。在近代，普氏野马原分布区从哈萨克斯坦的斋桑泊附近，向东穿过我国新疆维吾尔自治区北部的准噶尔盆地，至蒙古国阿尔泰山区及科布多河流域。目前国际上公认欧洲野马或称泰班野马是家马的祖先，但其已在 1897 年灭绝。从染色体数量上考虑，普氏野马的染色体数量为 2n=66，比家马多一对染色体，但普氏野马与家马可以繁殖可育后代，所以生活在亚洲东部的家马很可能有普氏野马的血统。

Equus ferus ssp. *przewalskii* once lived in China, and its scientific name was *Equus ferus* ssp. *przewalskii*. *Equus ferus* ssp. *przewalskii* was also known as Junggar wild horse. They were once widely distributed in the high-latitude grasslands and desert steppe zones in Eurasia. China was once the country of origin to the horse. In modern times, the original distribution area of the horse ran from near Zaysan Lake in Kazakhstan eastward across the Junggar Basin in the north of Xinjiang Uygur Autonomous Region to the Altai Mountains and Khovd River in Mongolia. Now Eurasian wild horses or tarpans are internationally recognized as ancestors of horses, but they were extinct in 1897. Considering the number of chromosomes, *Equus ferus* ssp. *przewalskii* as 2n=66 chromosomes, one pair more than horse. But the horse and a domesticated horse can breed offspring, so domesticated horses living in eastern Asia are likely to have blood relations with *Equus ferus* ssp. *przewalskii*.

普氏野马的野生自然种群在 20 世纪中叶灭绝。19 世纪末至 20 世纪初，西方人在蒙古国进行了 6 次普氏野马捕捉行动，最后一次是在 1903 年。他们将捕捉到的普氏野马运往欧洲，现存普氏野马大多是这些普氏野马的后代。目前，我国已从国外重新引入了一些普氏野马进行人工饲养繁殖，并已尝试将部分普氏野马在新疆和甘肃放归自然。

Equus ferus ssp. *przewalskii* was wiped out as a species in the middle of 20th century. From the late 19th century to the early 20th century, Westerners conducted 6 times of hunting activities in Mongolia, and the last hunting activity was in 1903. They shipped the captured horses to Europe, and the existing horses are mostly descendants of those from Mongolia. Now, China has introduced some horses from abroad for artificial breeding and reproduction, and has tried to release some of them into the wild in Xinjiang and Gansu.

4. 高鼻羚羊

4. *Saiga tatarica*

高鼻羚羊也叫赛加羚羊，是一种十分珍贵稀有的羚羊。我国传统中药中使用的羚羊角即是高鼻羚羊的角。我国是高鼻羚羊原产国之一，高鼻羚羊主要分布在新疆北部地区。由于栖息地破坏、过度狩猎等原因，我国高鼻羚羊大约在 20 世纪 40 — 50 年代灭绝。在国外，高鼻羚羊目前有数万只，主要分布于中亚半干旱地区，如俄罗斯卡尔梅克，哈萨克斯坦乌拉尔、乌斯秋尔特和别特帕克达尔，蒙古国西部中蒙边境附近。我国在 20 世纪 80 年代从国外重新引入了一些高鼻羚羊进行人工饲养繁殖，目的是在人工种群达到一定数量后放归自然。至 2016 年，在位于武威市的甘肃省濒危动物保护中心，高鼻羚羊人工种群数量已达近百只，并且在尝试将高鼻羚羊放归自然。

（陈建伟摄）
高鼻羚羊
Saiga tatarica (Credit: Chen Jianwei)

Saiga tatarica, also called as the saiga antelope, is a very rare antelope. The antelope horns used in traditional Chinese medicine are from *Saiga tatarica*. China is one of the countries of origin to *Saiga tatarica*, which was mainly distributed in the northern region of Xinjiang. Due to habitat destruction and over-hunting, *Saiga tatarica* was extinct in about 1940s and 1950s. In other countries, now there are tens of thousands of *Saiga tatarica*, mainly distributed in semi-arid regions of Central Asia, such as Kalmyk in Russia, Ural, Ustyurt and Betpak-Dala in Kazakhstan, and near the Sino-Mongolian border in western Mongolia. In the 1980s, China introduced some *Saiga tatarica* from abroad for artificial breeding and reproduction, for the purpose of releasing them into nature after the artificial population reached a certain number. By 2016, the artificial population of *Saiga tatarica* at the Protection Center of

Endangered Animals in Gansu Province had climbed up to nearly 100. And, China is trying to release these *Saiga tatarica* into the wild.

5. 犀牛

5. *Dicerorhinus*

　　犀牛是哺乳类犀科的总称，目前主要分布在非洲和东南亚，是最大的奇蹄目动物，也是当今体型仅次于大象的第二大陆地动物。头部有实心的独角或双角（有的雌性无角），起源于真皮，角脱落仍能复生。目前在非洲生活着两种犀牛——黑犀（非洲双角犀牛）和白犀（非洲大双角犀牛），在亚洲生活着三种犀牛——爪哇犀（亚洲独角犀牛）、印度犀（亚洲大独角犀牛）和苏门答腊犀（亚洲小双角犀牛）。目前全世界的犀牛可能仅有数万头，其中爪哇犀和苏门答腊犀濒临灭绝。造成犀牛日益减少的原因有盗猎、栖息地丧失和种群隔离等。犀牛的最大威胁是人类。由于国际市场还是对犀牛角有所需求，盗猎者因此可获得非常高的经济利益。在一些东亚国家，犀牛角被制成传统药材。阿拉伯国家把犀牛角看作社会级别的象征。在也门和阿曼，犀牛角被用来制作仪式上使用的匕首手柄。

Dicerorhinus is a general term for any mammal of the family Rhinocerotidae under the class Mammalia and is now mainly distributed in Africa and Southeast Asia. It is the largest odd-toed ungulate and the second largest land animal next to the elephant. Its head has a solid single horn or double horns (some females are hornless). The horn starts from the dermis and can be regenerated after shedding. Now, two species of rhinoceros live in Africa: *Diceros bicornis* (a rhinoceros with double horns in Africa) and *Ceratotherium simum* (a rhinoceros with large double horns in African); three species live in Asia: *Rhinoceros sondaicus* (a rhinoceros with a single horn in Asia), *Rhinoceros unicornis* (a rhinoceros with a large single horn in Asia), and *Dicerorhinus sumatrensis* (a rhinoceros with small double horns in Asian). Now, there may be only tens of thousands of *Dicerorhinus* in the world, and *Rhinoceros sondaicus* and *Dicerorhinus sumatrensis* are on the verge of extinction. Causes for the gradual decrease of *Dicerorhinus* include poaching, habitat loss, and population isolation. Humans are the biggest threat to *Dicerorhinus*. Due to the demand for rhino horns in the international market, poachers can obtain very high economic benefits from selling rhino horns. In some East Asian countries, rhino horns are made into traditional medicine. In Arab countries, rhino horns are considered as a symbol of social status. In Yemen and Oman, rhino horns are used to make dagger handles used on ceremonies.

　　在历史上，犀牛在我国曾广泛分布在南方各省，栖息在接近水源的林缘山地地带。唐朝时，在今湖南、湖北、广东、广西、四川、贵州甚至青海，都有分布。明朝时，只分布于现今贵州、云南。到了清朝时，仅分布于现今云南。由于人类的活动和过度开发，使得它们的栖息地逐年减少；再加上它们头部犀角的经济价值极高，使它们易受到人类的大肆猎杀，且离近代越近其被捕杀数量越多，20世纪初在中国几乎踪迹全无。1922年，随着最后一头小独角犀（爪哇犀）被猎杀，犀牛在中国彻底消失。

Historically, *Dicerorhinus* were widely distributed in the southern provinces of China, perching in the mountainous areas in the edge of forests near water source. During the Tang Dynasty, Hunan, Hubei, Guangdong, Guangxi, Sichuan, Guizhou, and even Qinghai had rhinoceros. During the Ming Dynasty, rhinoceros were only distributed in Guizhou and Yunnan. During the Qing Dynasty, they were only distributed in Yunnan. Due to human activities and overuse, their habitats were decreasing year by year; with high economic value of their head horns, they were vulnerable to rampant human hunting, and more and more *Dicerorhinus* were killed as recent modern times approached. By the early 20th century, they had almost vanished in China. In 1922, with the last small single-horned rhinoceros (*Rhinoceros sondaicus*) being hunted, *Dicerorhinus* disappeared completely from China.

第三节　我国野生动物保护工作任重道远
Section Ⅲ　Heavy Task of Wildlife Protection in China

你知道吗?
Do you know?

　　我国野生动物正面临着栖息地丧失或恶化、乱捕滥猎滥食、过度开发利用等严重威胁。

The wildlife in China is facing serious threats like habitat loss or deterioration, indiscriminate capturing and hunting, and overuse and over-utilization.

一、野生动物栖息地遭受破坏
I. Destruction of Wildlife Habitats

东北虎伤害家畜
a *Panthera tigris altaica* attacking livestock

伴随着以牺牲生态环境为代价的人类生产、生活及科技的进步，造成一些地区野生动物的栖息地面临着被蚕食、污染、破碎化等严重威胁。

The advances in human production, lives, and technology at the expense of the ecological environment have posed serious threats to wildlife habitats in some areas as they are being encroached upon, polluted, and fragmented.

人类较多活动侵占了一些野生动物的栖息地，造成人与野生动物的冲突呈多发态势。野生动物啃食庄稼、伤害人畜的事件经常发生。

Many of the human activities have encroached upon the habitats of some wildlife, causing frequent conflicts between humans and wildlife. Incidents of wildlife grazing crops and hurting livestock occur frequently.

随着我国人口增长和经济发展，对自然资源的需求不断增大，乱砍滥伐、过度放牧、不合理的围湖造田、沼泽开垦、过度利用土地和水资源，导致野生动物生存环境被破坏甚至消失，影响物种的正常生存。迅猛的城市化进程已把许多遥远的乡村连成一片，连续的大块自然生境被城市化所隔离。大规模的公路和铁路工程逐渐延伸到生物多样性比较丰富的山区和无人区，随之而来的是路旁大规模的森林采伐，阻断了野生动物的正常迁移和扩散过程，对野生动物的生存造成严重威胁。同时，原始的生态系统逐渐暴露在人类活动的影响下，造成生态系统的退化。随着我国经济的快速发展，城市化过程将成为我国广大农村未来发展的必然趋势，而大型工程建设将会越来越多，这些必然严重影响我国的生物多样性保护和生态环境的保护。

As the population and economy of China and the demand for natural resources grow, reckless illegal deforestation, overgrazing, irrational reclamation of land, swamp reclamation, and excessive use of land and water resources have destroyed and even ruined the habitats of wildlife, affecting the normal survival of species. The rapid urbanization has already connected many distant villages into one continuous chunk, making large contiguous natural habitats increasingly segmented in the process. Large-scale road and rail projects gradually extend to mountains and depopulated areas with rich biodiversity, followed by roadside massive deforestation, which blocks the normal migration and diffusion processes of wildlife and poses serious threats to the survival of wildlife. Meanwhile, the primitive ecosystems are gradually exposed to the impact of human activities and suffer degradation. With the rapid development of China's economy, the urbanization process will become the inevitable trend of future development in the vast rural areas in China, and there will be more and more large-scale construction projects. Inevitably, these will seriously affect the biodiversity conservation and ecological environment in China.

二、人与野生动物冲突增加
II. Increased Conflicts between Humans and Wildlife

由于一些地区野生动物栖息地人类活动较多，侵占了野生动物的栖息地，或者由于保护力度的加大，野生动物数量增加，造成人与野生动物的冲突也呈多发态势。经常发生野生动物啃食庄稼、伤害人畜的事件。

In the wildlife habitats of some areas, the habitats of wildlife are occupied by large numbers of human activities. Or with the increasing number of wildlife due to increased efforts to protect wildlife, more and more conflicts between humans and wildlife occur. Incidents of wildlife grazing crops and hurting livestock occur frequently.

近年来，生活在云南省境内的亚洲象肇事频繁，人与象开始发生冲突。在普洱市思茅区南屏镇、云仙乡，大象啃食庄稼地里的玉米、芭蕉，有时还会进入村寨觅食，

普洱市野象破坏庄稼
a wild elephant destroying crops in Pu'er City

推倒房屋。近十多年来，普洱市共有 8 人遭野象攻击致死，20 余人受伤。据统计，2009 年，在普洱市生活的野生动物共肇事 9420 起，致使 8 人受伤，造成经济损失 1093 万元人民币，其中亚洲象造成的损失就达 700 余万元。云南省林业主管部门已经启动了野生动物肇事补偿工作，普洱市还将亚洲象肇事纳入公共责任保险，减轻了亚洲象肇事给村民造成的损失。

In recent years, *Elephas maximuses* has frequently caused accidents in Yunnan Province, and conflicts between men and elephants started. In Yunxian Township, Nanping Town, Simao District, Pu'er City, elephants grazed corn and bananas on the cropland, and sometimes they went into the villages for food and tore down the houses there. Over the past decade, a total of 8 persons died from wild elephant attacks in Pu'er alone and more than 20 persons were injured. According to statistics, 9,420 accidents were caused by wildlife in Pu'er City in 2009, hurting 8 persons and generating RMB 10.93 million in economic losses, of which more than RMB 7 million was attributed to *Elephas maximuses*. The forestry authorities in Yunnan Province have started to compensate for wildlife accidents. In Pu'er City, Asian elephant-caused accidents are included in the public liability insurance to reduce the losses that the Asian elephant causes to the villagers.

近年来西藏不断加大自然保护区建设力度，野生动物资源储量比 20 年前增长 30% 以上。目前仅在那曲就有 1 万多头野牦牛、10 万多只藏羚羊、8 万多头藏野驴，比以往都有大幅度增加。随着草原上野生动物种群数量增加、活动频繁，"扰民"事件频频发生。主要"肇事者"包括棕熊、野牦牛、雪豹、岩羊等。西藏那曲县由恰乡一户牧民就遇到了一件尴尬事：一只棕熊趁自己不在家径直霸占了房屋，还拉开易拉罐喝起汽水来。由于不能猎杀棕熊，想尽办法也没能把它赶走，只能请县林业局工作人员帮忙处理。这是羌塘大草原上很多牧民遭遇的"烦心事"。2013 年那曲地区有

95%的乡镇遭遇过棕熊、狼、猞猁和雪豹等烈性动物的侵扰，累计损失近5万头（只）牲畜；还有3人被野生动物袭击死亡，其中包括一名十几岁的中学生，另有7人不同程度受伤。为此，西藏近年来积极实施野生动物"肇事"补偿机制，颁布实施了《西藏自治区重点陆生野生动物造成公民人身伤害和财产损失补偿暂行办法》，对野牦牛、棕熊等国家和自治区重点保护陆生野生动物造成的人身伤害和财产损失，政府给予不同程度的经济补偿。

In recent years, Tibet has been increasing its efforts to develop nature reserves, and its wildlife resources grew more than 30% over 20 years ago. Currently, there are more than 10,000 *Bos mutus*, more than 100,000 *Pantholops hodgsonii*, and more than 80,000 *Equus kiang* in Nagqu. All of the numbers increased significantly over the years. With the increased populations and increased activities of wildlife on the grasslands, they frequently "disturbed" residents. The main "perpetrators" includes *Ursus arctos*, *Bos mutus*, *Panthera uncia*, *Pseudois nayaur*, etc. A shepherd family in Youqia Village, Nagqu County, encountered an embarrassing incident: a *Ursus arctos* occupied the home while the shepherd was out, and the *Ursus arctos* opened the can to drink soda water. Because it was illegal to hunt *Ursus arctos*, they tried every method to expel it but failed. They had no choice but asked staff from the Forestry Bureau of the county for help. This was just one of the "troubles" that many shepherds living in Qiangtang Prairie suffered. In 2013, 95% of the villages in Nagqu experienced invasion of *Ursus arctos*, wolves, *Lynx lynx,* and *Panthera uncia*, losing nearly 50,000 livestock; 3 persons died from wild animal attacks, including a teenage student, and 7 persons were injured. For this reason, Tibet has actively implemented a compensation mechanism for "accidents" caused by wildlife in recent years and promulgated the *Interim Measures on Compensating Personal Injury and Property Damage of Citizens Caused by Key Terrestrial Wildlife in Tibet Autonomous Region* to make government economic compensation for any personal injury and property damage caused by key national and regional protected terrestrial wildlife such as *Bos mutus* and *Ursus arctos*.

三、乱捕滥猎滥食野生动物的情况时有发生
III. Occasional Illegal Reckless Capturing, Hunting and Eating of Wildlife

（一）乱捕滥猎野生动物
（Ⅰ）Reckless Illegal Capturing and Hunting of Wildlife

在候鸟迁徙季节，乱捕滥猎候鸟的现象时有发生，造成候鸟种类、数量逐年减少。在春、秋两季，在一些地区，不法分子利用候鸟选择当地作为越冬地或繁殖地、迁飞停歇地、迁飞通道、集群活动区等习性，采用网捕、强光照射、枪击等方式非法猎杀候鸟。

During the migratory seasons of migratory birds, over-hunting occurs to them frequently, leading to decreases in their variety and number year by year. In spring and autumn, in some areas, the criminals take advantage of the migratory birds' habits that they choose local area as their wintering grounds, breeding grounds, migratory stopover, migratory channels,and clustering areas to hunt them illegally by net, strong light exposure,gun, and other methods.

（二）滥食野生动物
（Ⅱ）Reckless Illegal Eating of Wildlife

1. 错误的消费观念亟须改变
1. Change the Wrong Consumption Concept

当前，对于滥食野生动物，国内部分人群的消费习惯和观念仍然没有和建设生态文明的时代要求同步发展，一部分人抱着吃野味滋补的错误想法，另外还有猎奇性的消费、炫耀式的消费。这些都是亟须改变的错误观念。

Currently, for the problem of reckless illegal eating of wildlife, the consumption habit and concept of some people in the country fails to catch up with the requirements of developing ecological civilization. Some people still hold the misconception of obtaining nutrients from eating wildlife, while others commit to novelty-seeking and conspicuous consumption. These are misconceptions that need to be changed.

2. 滥食野生动物危害人类健康
2. Reckless Illegal Eating of Wildlife Harms the Health of People

滥食野生动物的特征，是吃食的野生动物为非法来源或来源不明，或者来源明确但是非法获得，或者来源合法却没有按规定进行检验检疫，或者吃食的是毒杀的野生动物，或者吃食的是以不文明方式处死的野生动物。野生动物很可能会携带对人体有害甚至危害十分严重的病毒、细菌等微生物，所以滥食野生动物不仅仅破坏和影响野生动物资源、危及生态安全，严重损害我国的国家和公民形象，同时还可能危害人类健康。人民日报记者在2013年4月1日的报道中向社会发出呼吁，"为了人类自身的生命健康，请不要滥食野生动物。"这一呼吁得到了社会各界人士的积极响应。

There are some typical features of reckless and illegal eating: people eat wild animals with illegal or unknown source, or with clear source but illegally obtained, or with legal source but without prescriptive inspection and quarantine, or with poisoned wildlife, or with the uncivilized way to be killed. The reporter of People's Daily appealed to our society in the reporting: "Stop eating wild animals for the health of human life" in April 1, 2003. This appeal has received a positive response from all sectors of society.

3. 要把非法滥食野生动物和合法、科学利用野生动物区分开来

3. Illegal Eating of Wildlife Should Be Distinguished from Legal and Scientific Use of Wildlife

保护野生动物，但不能误导为极端保护主义。实际上，到目前还几乎没有哪个国家宣布不能吃食野生动物。关键是要合法、科学。如：人工养殖的鹿类、雉类、鳄类是可以吃的；在美国每年狩猎野鸭达 2000 万只，也是可以吃的。要把非法滥食野生动物和合法、科学利用野生动物区分开来。当然，要考虑野生动物疫病问题，关键是要进行检疫检验。如果不经检疫检验，猪、牛、羊等也同样可能存在食用安全问题。

The protection of wildlife should not be misunderstood as extreme protectionism. In fact, there are hardly any countries that have announced it is illegal to eat wildlife. The key is to eat them legally and scientifically. For example, artificially raised deer, pheasants, and crocodiles are edible; in the United States, 20 million wild ducks are hunted each year and they are edible too. Illegal eating of wildlife should be distinguished from the legal and scientific use of wildlife. Of course, the key to the issue of wildlife diseases is to conduct quarantine inspection. Without quarantine inspection, pigs, cattle and sheep may also have food safety problems.

四、野生动物保护任重道远
IV. Heavy Task of Wildlife Protection

（一）野生动物保护工作任务重难度大
（ I ）Heavy and Difficult Task of Wildlife Protection

我国野生动物保护任重道远主要表现在以下四个方面：一是我国野生动物种类多、分布范围广，且大多位于偏远落后区域；二是社会上还存在一些不健康的滥食、滥用野生动物的陋习，公众保护意识有待提高；三是保护与资源开发利用之间的冲突日益激烈，不仅城市扩张、道路建设、农业开垦、环境污染等给野生动物栖息地保护带来巨大压力，并且对野生动物资源的开发利用压力也越来越大；四是由于底子薄、长期投入少，导致机构不健全、人员力量薄弱、设施设备落后，基层保护能力严重不足，难以胜任繁重的保护任务。

The difficulty of the task of protecting wildlife in China is mainly reflected in the following four respects: First, the wildlife in China include numerous varieties and is distributed widely, mostly in remote and backward areas; second, there are still some bad habits of eating and abusing wildlife unhealthily and recklessly in society, and the public awareness of wildlife protection needs to be heightened; third, the conflict between resource conservation and resource development and utilization becomes increasingly acute, and urban expansion, road construction, agricultural reclamation, and environmental pollution bring not only great pressure on the protection of wildlife habitats but also increasing stress on the exploitation and utilization of wildlife resources; four, due to a weak foundation and few long-term investments, there are such problems as incomplete institutions, weak staffing, poor facilities and equipment, and seriously inadequate protection ability at the grassroots level, thereby making it extremely difficult to assume the daunting heavy protection task.

（二）野生动物保护是一项长期工作
（Ⅱ）Protection of Wildlife as a Long-term Cause

目前，我国正在继续扩大自然保护区建设，并通过扩大人工繁育，改善濒危野生动物生境，强化野外巡护等措施，阻止濒危物种的增加。同时，严格禁止对濒危野生动物资源进行直接的商业利用和以食用为目的的猎捕行为。对盗猎、非法走私野生动物制品等行为进行严厉打击，加大濒危野生动物贸易管理执法力度以规范市场管理。对野生动物保护工作要常抓不懈。

At present, China is continuing to expand the construction of nature reserves and prevent the increase in the number of endangered species by expanding artificial breeding of endangered wildlife, improving their habitats, and strengthening field patrol. At the same time, direct commercial utilization of endangered wildlife resources and hunting them for food are strictly prohibited. Poaching and smuggling of wildlife products are severely punished, and the management of and the law enforcement around trade in endangered wildlife must be strengthened in order to regulate the market management. The protection of wildlife should be enforced unremittingly.

研究性学习
Investigative Study

同学们，你吃过野生动物吗？谈谈人们为什么选择进食野生动物。
Have you ever eaten any wildlife? Explain why people choose to eat wildlife.

拓展阅读
Extended Reading

新闻报道——滥食野生动物危害人体健康
News Report — Reckless Illegal Eating of Wildlife Harms Human Health

　　尽管国家三令五申，有关执法部门加大打击售食野生动物行为力度，但滥食野生动物甚至是珍稀野生动物现象仍然屡禁不止。专家指出，滥食野生动物不仅破坏生态环境，对人体健康也可构成巨大威胁。

Despite the repeated orders of the state and the increased effort at cracking down on the sale and eating of wildlife by relevant law enforcement agencies, reckless illegal eating of wildlife and even rare wildlife still exists. Experts point out that eating wildlife recklessly not only destroys the environment, but also poses a huge threat to human health.

　　蛇是一些人常食的野生动物，但专家在蛇身上发现多种对人体有害的寄生虫。以人们常食的榕蛇为例，专家在蛇的皮下、肌肉内和腹腔中发现了大量的寄生虫。这种寄生虫经实验室鉴定为"曼氏迭宫绦虫"的幼虫——裂头蚴，一旦进入人体内，即可使人感染裂头蚴病，引起眼、口腔、皮下、脑及内脏各部的疾病。裂头蚴在肠道内发育为成虫，即曼氏迭宫绦虫，可导致腹部不适，恶心呕吐，严重时危及生命。蛇胆虽是一味中药，但其药用与食用迥然不同。药用蛇胆的来源、炮制方式、服用方法和用量都有严格精确的规定。而餐桌上的蛇胆，讲究个"鲜"字，都是从蛇腹中现取的。上海市长征医院中医科主任魏品康说："鲜蛇胆里面虽含有促进消化的成分，但也含有许多由肝脏输出的有毒物质乃至尖吻蝮蛇舌状虫（鞭节舌虫）等寄生虫。盲目吞服鲜蛇胆，极易损害体内器官，诱发肝、肾功能衰竭。"

Snake is a common wild animal viewed as food by some people. However, experts found many harmful parasites in snakes. Take *Ptyas korros* that people usually eat as an example. Experts found a large number of parasites under the skin and inside the muscle and abdominal cavity of the snake. The parasites were identified in laboratory as larvae of "*Spirometra mansoni*". The larvae, called *Plerocercoid*, can make people infected with sparganosis and further cause diseases in eyes, mouth, skin, brain and internal organs once they go into the human body. *Plerocercoid* can develop into worms, i.e. *Spirometra mansoni*, in the intestine and cause abdominal discomfort, nausea and vomiting, and even threaten life in serious cases. Although the snake gall is a kind of Chinese medicine, its functions as a medicine and as food are totally different. Sources, processing methods, and taking method and dose of medicinal snake gall are all strictly prescribed. However, the snake galls served on the dining table are valuable for its "freshness" and thus are usually directly taken from the belly of the snake. Wei Pinkang, director of the Department of Chinese Medicine in Shanghai Changzheng Hospital, said, "Although fresh snake galls contain ingredients that promote digestion, they also contain many toxic substances from the liver and even parasites like *Armillifer agkistrodontis*. Swallowing fresh snake gall blindly is likely to damage organs in the body and induce liver or kidney failure."

动物疾病专家华育平教授指出：灵长类动物、啮齿类动物、兔形类动物、有蹄类动物、鸟类等多种野生动物与人的共患疾病有 100 多种，如狂犬病、结核、B 病毒、鼠疫、炭疽、甲肝等。此外，专家指出，当前人们食用的野生动物，大多数生存环境不明、来源不明，卫生检疫部门又难以进行有效监控，许多疾病的病原体就在对野生动物的猎捕、运输、饲养、宰杀、储存、加工和食用过程中扩散、传播。工业"三废"，生活污水、污物，杀虫、灭鼠药等高残留的农药对环境污染加剧，也对野生动物造成毒害，人吃了这种环境下的野生动物就更有中毒的可能。更有甚者，一些偷猎者常常采取毒杀的方法获取野生动物，而且采用的毒药毒性大，不易降解，残留在被毒杀动物体内，食用这样的动物就有被继续毒害的危险。

According to Professor Hua Yuping, an animal disease expert, primates, rodents, lagomorphs, ungulates, birds, etc. share more than 100 zoonotic diseases with humans, such as rabies, tuberculosis, B virus, plague, anthrax, and hepatitis. In addition, the expert pointed out that the wildlife that people eat now mostly come from unknown living environments and unknown sources, making it difficult for the health and quarantine departments to carry out effective monitoring. Pathogens of many diseases diffuse and spread during the hunting, transporting, breeding, slaughtering, storage, processing and consumption processes of wildlife. The waste gas, waste water and industrial residue, sewage, dirt, pesticides, rodenticides, and other high-residue pesticides exacerbate the environmental pollution and poison the wildlife. People will be more likely to be poisoned if they eat wildlife growing up under such environments. What's worse, some poachers often killed wildlife with poison and use highly toxic poisons that are resistant to degradation, leaving the poison inside the dead animals. Eating such animals brings the risk of being further poisoned.

中国科学院动物研究所研究员冯祚建、中国野生动物保护协会原秘书长陈润生严厉批评了一些人的饮食陋习。他们说，现在吃奇、吃特已经成为一部分人追求的"时尚"，甚至被看作是身份的象征。再加上"药补不如食补"的片面认识，很多人相信野生动物的食补作用，导致滥食野生动物。营养专家在对家禽、家畜和几种野生动物的营养分析比较中发现，它们在蛋白质、糖类、能量等主要指标上相差无几。

Feng Zuojian, a researcher at the Institute of Zoology in the Chinese Academy of Sciences, and Chen Runsheng, former Secretary-General of China Wildlife Conservation Association, severely criticized the poor diet habits of some people. They said that eating something novel and special has become a "fashion" and even a status symbol pursued by some people. This, coupled with the misbelief in the saying "Food cures better than medicine", led many people to believe in the dietetic invigoration of wildlife and eat wildlife indiscriminately. Through analyzing and comparing the nutrition of poultry, livestock and several wild animals, nutrition experts found that they are almost the same in main indicators like protein, carbohydrates, and energy.

(《人民日报》2003 年 04 月 02 日第 11 版：http://www.people.com.cn/GB/huanbao/57/20030402/960621.html)

(*People's Daily*, Page 11 in the April 2, 2003, issue: http://www.people.com.cn/GB/huanbao/57/20030402/960621.html)

第三章　我国野生动物保护措施和保护等级标准

Chapter Ⅲ　Measures and Grading Standard of Wildlife Protection in China

对野生动物的保护是一项长期繁复的工作。这项工作的进行不但需要先进的技术和有效的管理手段，更需要在法律、行政、宣传、财经、科研、教育等多个领域、多个部门共同配合、全民参与来共同完成。

The protection of wildlife is a long complicated task. This task not only requires advanced technology and efficient management means, but also needs cooperation and participation of multiple fields and multiple departments in law, administration, publicity, finance, scientific research, education, etc.

第一节　法律保障

Section Ⅰ　Legal Protection

你知道吗？

Do you know?

早在 1988 年，《中华人民共和国野生动物保护法》中就确立了国家对野生动物进行保护的方针，即：加强资源保护，积极驯养繁殖，合理开发利用。

As early as 1988, the *Law of the People's Republic of China on the Protection of Wildlife* put forward the national guideline in wildlife protection, namely: strengthening resource conservation, actively domesticating and breeding animals, and rationally developing and utilizing animal resources.

一、我国有关野生动物保护的政策与法规
I. Policies and Laws about Wildlife Protection in China

目前我国已初步建立了以《野生动物保护法》《森林法》《陆生野生动物保护实施条例》《水生野生动物保护实施条例》《濒危野生动植物进出口管理条例》《自然保护区条例》等为核心的野生动物保护法律法规体系，结合野生动物保护地方性法规，力图从完善立法、强化执法、强化公众的宣传教育等多个方面来完善野生动物保护的长效机制。

Now, China has initially established a legal system for the protection of wildlife, covering the *Law on the Protection of Wildlife, Forest Law, Regulations on Implementing the Protection of Terrestrial Wildlife, Regulations for the Implementation of Wild Aquatic Animal Protection, Regulations on Administration of Import and Export of Endangered Wild Animals and Plants*, and *Regulations of Natural Reserves* at the core. This system, combined with local laws and regulations on wildlife protection, is intended to improve the long-term wildlife protection mechanism from multiple aspects of perfected legislation, law enforcement, and strengthened public advocacy and education.

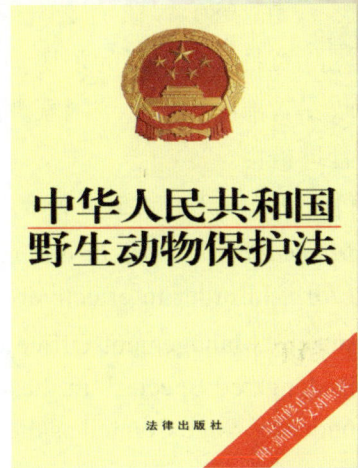

《中华人民共和国野生动物保护法》
Law of the People's Republic of China on the Protection of Wildlife

二、我国参与的与野生动物保护相关的主要国际公约
Ⅱ. Major International Conventions that China Joined for Wildlife Protection

我国积极参与国际野生动物保护行动。相关国际公约、协定等是国与国之间联合行动的保护形式，也是野生动物保护行动实施的依据或协调机制。

China is active in participating in international wildlife protection actions. Signing international conventions and agreements is a form of joint protection actions among countries and a basis or coordination mechanism to jointly implement wildlife protection actions.

1. 濒危野生动植物种国际贸易公约

1. Convention on International Trade in Endangered Species of Wild Fauna and Flora

在 1980 年 12 月 25 日我国加入了《濒危野生动植物种国际贸易公约》。为了切实履行公约，我国在国务院林业行政主管部门设立了"国家濒危物种进出口管理办公室"作为管理机构。

On December 25, 1980, China joined *Convention on International Trade in Endangered Species of Wild Fauna and Flora*. In order to effectively implement the convention, China set up "Management Office of Import and Export of National Endangered Species" in the forestry administrative department under the State Council as the governing body.

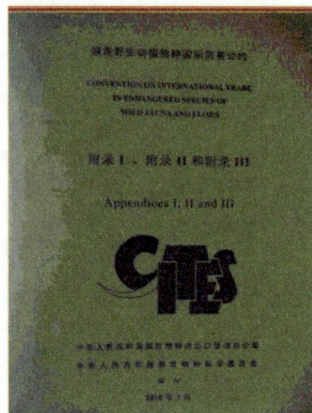

《濒危野生动植物种国际贸易公约》
Convention on International Trade in Endangered Species of Wild Fauna and Flora

2. 生物多样性公约

2. Convention on Biological Diversity

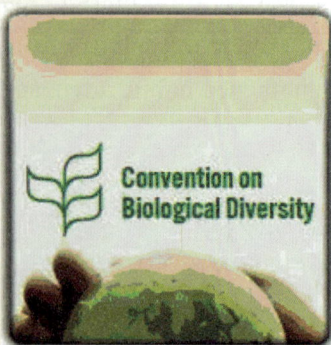

《生物多样性公约》
Convention on Biological Diversity

1992 年 6 月联合国在巴西召开环境及发展大会通过了《生物多样性公约》，我国成为签字国，由国务院环境保护行政主管部门负责牵头履约，对保护生物多样性给予了相当关注。

In June 1992, *Convention on Biological Diversity* was adopted at the United Nations Conference on Environment and Development (UNCED) in Brazil. China is a signatory country, and the environmental protection administrative department of the State Council is responsible for implementation of the convention, thus paying due attention on the conservation of biological diversity.

3. 关于特别是作为水禽栖息地的国际重要湿地公约

3. Convention on Wetlands of International Importance Especially as Waterfowl Habitat

《关于特别是作为水禽栖息地的国际重要湿地公约》（简称《湿地公约》）于 1971 年 2 月 2 日在伊朗拉姆萨尔签订，于 1975 年 12 月 21 日正式生效，目前已成为国际上重要的自然保护公约，受到各国政府的重视。我国于 1992 年加入该公约，目前该公约已经成为我国湿地类型自然保护区建设和管理的重要指南。

Convention on Wetlands of International Importance Especially as Waterfowl Habitat (referred to as *the Ramsar Convention on Wetlands*) was signed in Ramsar, Iran on February 2, 1971 and came into force on December 21, 1975. Now it has become an important international convention on nature conservation and receives much attention of all governments from different countries. China joined the convention in 1992, and the convention now has become an important guideline for China to develop and manage wetland nature reserves.

4. 其他条约或协定
4. Other Conventions or Agreements

我国还加入了其他一些与野生动物保护相关的国际条约，如《联合国防治荒漠化公约》《保护世界文化和自然遗产公约》等。部分协定如：1981 年 3 月 3 日，我国政府与日本政府签订《保护候鸟及其栖息环境协定》；1986 年 10 月 20 日，我国政府与澳大利亚政府签订《保护候鸟及其栖息环境的协定》；1990 年 5 月 6 日，我国政府与蒙古国政府签订《关于保护自然环境的合作协定》等。

China has also joined a number of other international conventions releted to wildlife protection, such as *UN Convention to Combat Desertification* and *Convention Concerning the Protection of the World Cultural and Natural Heritage*. Some of the agreements included: *Sino-Japan Agreement on Protection of Migratory Birds and Their Habitat Environment*, signed by the Chinese government and the Japanese government on March 3, 1981; *Sino-Australia Agreement on Protection of Migratory Birds and Their Habitat Environment*, signed by the Chinese government and the Australian government on October 20, 1986; *Sino-Mengolian Cooperation Agreement on the Protection of Natural Environment*, signed by the Chinese and Mongolian governments on May 6, 1990.

涉及野生动物保护的国际条约还有很多，如《保护迁徙野生动物物种公约》《保护南极海洋生物资源公约》《保护南极海豹公约》《保护北极熊协定》等。有些涉及野生动物保护的国际公约或协定我国还暂未加入。

There are many other international conventions concerning wildlife protection, such as *Convention on the Conservation of Migratory Species of Wild Animals, Convention on the Conservation of Antarctic Marine Living Resources, Convention on the Conservation of Antarctic Seals, Agreement on the Conservation of Polar Bears*, etc. There are some other international conventions or agreements concerning wildlife protection that China has not yet joined.

拓展阅读
Extended Reading

制约野生动物保护几大难题
Several Major Problems to Restrict Wildlife Protection

2013 年 06 月 24 日 07：17：03　来源：新华每日电讯
June 24, 2013, at 07:17:03　Source: Xinhua Daily Telegraph

经过多年的努力，一些地区的野生动植物保护与自然保护区管理取得了显著的成效，但是个别地方，乱捕滥猎现象时有发生，非法捕杀、贩运野生动物现象仍旧存在。特别是几大难题制约着野生动物保护工作的进一步开展。

After years of efforts, remarkable achievements have been made in the wild flora and fauna protection and management of nature reserves in some areas. However, reckless hunting still occurs occasionally in other places and illegal hunting and trafficking wildlife still exist. In particular, several major problems below restrict the further advancement of wildlife protection.

第一，保护管理体系还需不断完善。到目前为止，一些地区还有不少极小种群野生动植物分布区、自然保护区等没有设立专门的保护管理机构；还有很多地方虽然成立了保护管理机构，但没有编制、没有专职人员、没有经费保障等，工作根本开展不起来。

Firstly, the protection and management system needs to be improved constantly. So far, there are many distribution areas of small wild flora and fauna populations and natural reserves in some places that do not have a special protection and management agency; in other areas, although there are protection and management agencies, they do not have permanent or full-time staff and nor are they supported by funding guarantee. Thus, it is impossible for them to perform any work.

第二，保护资金投入严重不足。很多自然保护区处于偏远落后地区，保护任务十分繁重。但在保护资金方面，投入力度与保护难度极不相称。

Secondly, there is a serious shortage of funds, supporting nature conservation. Many nature reserves are located in remote and backward areas with daunting protection tasks. However, the protection funds are ill-matched to the real need to work.

第三,保护与开发利用的矛盾日益尖锐。随着城镇化、工业化的快速推进和大型建设项目的实施,物种栖息地和生态系统受到的威胁日益增大,环境污染、生物资源过度利用和无序开发对野生动植物和自然生态系统的影响加剧。特别是当自然保护区影响到地方经济发展,保护与开发利用的冲突就必然升级,而一些基层地方领导对保护工作认识不足,存在重开发轻保护的现象。

Thirdly, the conflict between protection and exploitation becomes increasingly acute. With the rapid advancement of urbanization and industrialization and the implementation of large-scale construction projects, species habitats and ecosystems are more and more threatened. Environmental pollution and over-exploitation and disorderly development of biological resources have intensified effects on wildlife and natural ecosystems. Especially when nature reserves affect local economic development, the conflict between protection and exploitation is bound to upgrade. However, because some of the grassroots local leaders have poor awareness of the protection task, they tend to weigh development over protection.

第四,法制建设和执法监管有待进一步加强。例如,某省现行的保护野生动植物的法律法规主要制定于20世纪80 — 90年代,难以预见到现阶段保护管理工作出现的新问题、新情况。此外,还存在行政许可审核标准模糊、要求不明确等问题。同时,诸多科技瓶颈制约着保护管理水平的提高。

Fourthly, the legal system construction and the law enforcement supervision need to be further strengthened. For example, the existing laws and regulations on wildlife protection in one province were mainly enacted in the 1980s and the 1990s, making it difficult to foresee new problems and new trends appearing in the protection and management work under current stage. In addition, there are problems like vague standards and unclear requirements of administrative licensing approval. Meanwhile, many technological bottlenecks restrict the improvement of the protection and management level.

第二节　野生动物就地保护和迁地保护
Section Ⅱ　In-situ Protection and Ex-situ Protection of Wildlife

你知道吗?
Do you know?

就地保护是指为了保护生物多样性,把包含保护对象在内的一定面积的陆地或水体划分出来,进行保护和管理。就地保护主要指建立自然保护区。

In-situ protection refers to the protection and management of a certain area of land or waters including the protected objects for the sake of biological diversity protection. In-situ protection is mainly about building nature reserves.

迁地保护是指为了保护生物多样性，把因生存条件不复存在，物种数量极少或难以找到配偶等原因，其生存和繁衍受到严重威胁的物种迁出原地，移入动物园、野生动物园、植物园、水族馆或濒危动物繁育中心，进行特殊的保护和管理。

Ex-situ protection refers to the special protection and management of species that are relocated from their places of origins into zoos, wildlife parks, aquariums or endangered animal breeding centers because their survival and reproduction are seriously threatened by the loss of survival conditions, extremely limited number of species, or difficulty in finding mates, for the sake of biological diversity protection.

一、自然保护区
I. Nature Reserves

1. 我国自然保护区内部功能区划
1. Division of Internal Functions of Nature Reserves in China

根据自然保护区内不同区域的功能，我国自然保护区的内部区划可分为三个区域：核心区、缓冲区和实验区。

According to different functions of the areas within nature reserves, the internal areas of nature reserves in China can be divided into three zones: core zone, buffer zone, and experimental zone.

2. 我国自然保护区的类型
2. Categories of Nature Reserves in China

根据自然保护区的主要保护对象，可将自然保护区划分为9个类型：森林生态系统类型、草原与草甸生态系统类型、荒漠生态系统类型、内陆湿地和水域生态系统类型、海洋和海岸生态系统类型、野生动物类型、野生植物类型、地质遗迹类型、古生物遗迹类型。有些自然保护区包括了多个类型。

According to the main protection targets, nature reserves can be divided into nine categories: forest ecosystem, grassland and meadow ecosystem, desert ecosystem, inland wetland and water ecosystem, marine and coastal ecosystem, wild fauna, wild flora, geological relics, and paleontological remains. Some nature reserves may include several categories.

3. 我国自然保护区等级标准
3. Grading Standard of Nature Reserves in China

我国的自然保护区分为国家级自然保护区和地方级自然保护区。地方级自然保护区又可分为省（自治区、直辖市）级自然保护区、市（州、地区）级自然保护区和县级自然保护区。

Nature reserves in China are divided into national nature reserves and local nature reserves. Local nature reserves can be further divided into provincial (autonomous region and municipal) nature reserves, city-level (state, regional) and county-level nature reserves.

二、野生动物迁地保护机构
Ⅱ. Ex-situ Wildlife Protection Agencies

1. 动物园
1. Zoos

动物园是最早的野生动物展示和迁地保护机构。我国的动物园和公园动物展区目前已有数百个。比较著名的动物园有北京动物园、上海动物园等。

Zoos are the earliest display and ex-situ protection agencies of wildlife. Now there are hundreds of zoos and animal parks in China. The famous ones include Beijing Zoo and Shanghai Zoo.

2. 野生动物园
2. Wildlife Parks

野生动物园在国外通常是指开放式的动物园或狩猎公园，也包括一些国家的国家公园，是野生动物迁地保护的一种重要形式。在我国，一般认为那些利用自然环境或人工模拟环境开放式驯养及展出野生动物的综合性场所即为野生动物园。自1993年原林业部批准建立全国第一家野生动物园——深圳野生动物园投入运营以来，截止到2010年年底全国已有野生动物园34家。包括北京野生动物园、北京八达岭野生动物园、上海野生动物园、杭州野生动物世界、哈尔滨北方森林动物园、碧峰峡野生动物园、广东长隆野生动物世界、重庆野生动物园、秦皇岛野生动物园、沈阳森林野生动物园、新疆天山野生动物园、西安秦岭野生动物园等。

Wildlife parks usually refer to open zoos or hunting parks abroad, including national parks in some countries. They are an important form of ex-situ protection of wildlife. In China, it is generally believed that complexes where wildlife is domesticated and displayed in an open way by using natural environment or artificial environment are considered as wildlife parks. Since Safari Park Shenzhen, the former Ministry of Forestry approved the establishment of the first wildlife park in the country, was put into operation in 1993, there had been 34 wildlife parks in the country by the end of 2010, including Beijing Wildlife Park, Beijing Badaling Wildlife Park, Shanghai Wild Animal Park, Hangzhou Safari Park, Harbin Northern Forest Zoo, Bifengxia Safari Park, Guangdong Chimelong Safari Park, Chongqing Safari Park, Qinhuangdao Wildlife Park, Shenyang Forest Safari Park, Xinjiang Tianshan Safari Park, and Xi'an Qinling Wildlife Park,etc.

北京野生动物园于 2001 年 8 月正式开园，目前实际用地面积为 240 公顷（3600 亩），距离北京市 42 千米，有动物 200 多种、10000 余头（只）。园内设有散放观赏区、步行观赏区、动物观赏娱乐区、科普教育区、儿童动物园和游乐园等，建有主题动物场、馆 30 多个。

Beijing Wildlife Park was opened in August 2001 and now covers an area of 240 hectares(3,600 mu), 42 km from Beijing. It has more than 10,000 animals in 200 varieties. In the park, there are free viewing zone, walking viewing zone, animal viewing and entertainment zone, popular science and education zone, children's zoo, and amusement parks, as well as over 30 animal theme venues.

上海野生动物园于 1995 年 11 月正式开园，展区占地 153 公顷，距上海市中心约 35 千米，属 5A 级景区，有珍稀动物 200 余种，上万余头（只），分建动物表演馆、猛兽区、食草动物区、圈养动物区、其他动物展区。

Shanghai Wild Animal Park was opened in November 1995, covering an area of 153 hectares, about 35 km from Shanghai. The project is a 5A level scenic spot where there are more than 10,000 rare animals in 200 species. It includes animal show venue, beast zone, herbivore zone, captive animal zone, and other animal zone.

杭州野生动物世界于 2002 年 4 月正式开园，总面积 267 公顷（4000 亩），为 4A 级景区，号称华东地区规模最大。距离杭州市 15 千米，有动物近 200 多种、10000 余头（只）。杭州野生动物世界是华东地区唯一可自己驾驶入园游览的大型野生动物主题公园。

Hangzhou Safari Park was opened in April 2002, covering an area of 267 hectares(4,000 mu). It is a 4A level scenic spot and is claimed as the largest safari park in East China. It is 15 km from Hangzhou and has more than 10,000 animals in nearly 200 species. Hangzhou Safari Park is the only large wildlife theme park that allows visitors to drive in the park in East China.

哈尔滨北方森林动物园于 2004 年 9 月正式开园，位于阿城市的鸽子洞地区，园区面积 848 公顷，在国内野生动物园中占地面积最大，驯养动物共计 240 余种 5000 余只（头），距离哈尔滨市 46 千米，森林覆盖率达 95.8% 以上，园林与自然景观浑然一体，被大山环抱。

Located in Gezidong, Acheng City, Harbin Northern Forest Zoo was opened in September 2004 and covers an area of 848 hectares, the largest area among domestic wildlife parks. It domesticates a total of 5,000 animals in more than 240 species. It is 46 km from Harbin. With a forest coverage rate of more than 95.8%, the gardens and natural landscape are melted seamlessly and surrounded by mountains in the zoo.

3. 水族馆
3. Aquariums

近年来，随着经济社会的发展，国民生活水平的提高，一些城市纷纷兴建海洋馆或者极地馆。2002 年大连老虎滩海洋公园极地馆的建成开放，将"海洋馆"的概念延伸到"极地"。目前，我国的水族馆主要有：青岛水族馆、香港海洋公园、中国科学院水生生物研究所白鱀豚馆、徐州云龙湖水上世界、大连圣亚海洋世界、福州左海海底世界、南京海底世界、北京工体富国海底世界、广州海洋馆、厦门海底世界、北京太平洋海底世界、秦皇岛新澳海底世界、北京海洋馆、上海长风海洋世界、深圳小梅沙海洋世界、长沙海底世界、屏东海洋生物博物馆、北海海底世界、南宁海底世界、乌鲁木齐盛贝特海洋馆、上海海洋水族馆、太原迎泽公园海底世界、大连老虎滩海洋公园、长沙动物园海豚馆、武汉东湖海洋世界、花莲远雄海洋公园、青岛海底世界、桂林海洋世界、郑州海洋馆、南昌海洋公园、重庆兴澳海底世界、山海关乐岛海洋公园、蓬莱海洋极地世界、洛阳龙门海洋馆、西安曲江海洋公园、哈尔滨极地馆、抚顺皇家极地海洋世界、青岛极地海洋世界、宁波海洋世界、杭州极地海洋公园、成都海洋馆。

In recent years, with the economic and social development and the improvement of national living standards, aquariums or polar museums have been built in some cities. The construction and opening of the Polar Museum in 2002 in Dalian Laohutan Ocean Park extended the concept of "aquarium" to "Polar". At present, the aquariums in China mainly include: Qingdao Aquarium, Hong Kong Ocean Park, Baiji Dolphin Museum of Institute of Hydrobiology of Chinese Academy of Sciences, Xuzhou Yunlonghu Water Park, Dalian Sun Asia Ocean World, Fuzhou Zuohai Sea World, Nanjing Sea World, Fuguo Sea World in Workers' Stadium of Beijing, Guangzhou Ocean World, Xiamen Sea World, Beijing Pacific Sea World, Qinhuangdao Xin'ao Sea World, Beijing Aquarium, Shanghai Changfeng Ocean World, Shenzhen Xiaomeisha Sea World, Changsha Sea World, Pingtung Museum of Marine Biology and Aquarium, Beihai Sea World, Nanning Sea World, Urumqi Shengbeite

Aquarium, Shanghai Ocean Aquarium, Taiyuan Sea World of Yingze Park, Dalian Laohutan Ocean Park, Dolphinarium of Changsha Zoo, Wuhan Donghu Ocean World, Hualian Farglory Ocean Park, Qingdao Underwater World, Guilin Sea World, Zhengzhou Aquarium, Nanchang Ocean Park, Chongqing Xing'ao Underwater World, Shanhaiguan Ledao Ocean Park, Penglai Ocean Polar World, Luoyang Longmen Aquarium, Xi'an Qujiang Ocean Park, Harbin Polar Museum, Fushun Royal Polar Ocean World, Qingdao Polar Ocean World, Ningbo Ocean World, Hangzhou Polar Ocean Park, and Chengdu Aquarium.

研究性学习
Investigative Study

同学们，请为我们介绍一个你游览过而大家未见的动物园吧。

Please introduce a zoo that you visit but not known to others.

拓展阅读
Extended Reading

我国自然保护区之最
Top Nature Reserves in China

1. 我国建立最早的自然保护区

1. Earliest Nature Reserve in China

我国于 1956 年在广东省肇庆市的鼎湖山，建立了第一个自然保护区——鼎湖山自然保护区。鼎湖山国家级自然保护区总面积约 11.33 平方千米，位于广东省肇庆市鼎湖区，距离广州市西南 100 千米，主要保护对象为南亚热带地带性森林植被类型——季风常绿阔叶林及其丰富的生物多样性。保护区内生物多样性丰富，是华南地区生物多样性最富集的地区之一，被生物学家称为"物种宝库"和"基因储存库"。

The first nature reserve, Dinghushan Nature Reserve, was built in Dinghushan, Zhaoqing City, Guangdong Province, in 1956. Dinghushan National Nature Reserve covers a total area of about 11.33 km^2, located in Dinghu District, Zhaoqing City, Guangdong Province, and 100 km to the southwest of Guangzhou City. The main protection targets are monsoon evergreen broad-leaved forest and its rich biodiversity of zonal forest and vegetation types in south subtropics. The rich biological diversity in the nature reserve makes the district one of the areas with the richest biodiversity in southern China and is named by biologists as "treasure of species" and "genetic repository".

2. 我国面积最大的自然保护区
2. Largest Nature Reserve in China

西藏的羌塘自然保护区是我国面积最大的自然保护区，面积达 29.8 万平方千米。保护区位于西藏自治区的那曲地区和阿里地区，于 1993 年经西藏自治区人民政府批准建立，于 2000 年 4 月被国务院批准为国家级自然保护区。是一个以高原生态系统和珍稀野生动物为主要保护对象的自然保护区。主要保护对象为保存完整的、独特的高寒生态系统及多种大型有蹄类动物。保护区内有国家一级保护野生动物雪豹、藏羚、西藏野驴、野牦牛等分布。

Changtang Nature Reserve in Tibet is the largest nature reserve in China. With an area of 298,000 km^2, it is located in Nagqu and Ngari in Tibet Autonomous Region. The nature reserve was founded with the approval of the People's Government Tibet Autonomous Region in 1993 and was approved as a national nature reserve by the State Council in April 2000. It is a nature reserve that protects plateau ecosystems and rare wildlife. The main protection targets are completely preserved and unique alpine ecosystems and a variety of large ungulates. The nature reserve is home to national first-grade protected wildlife such as *Panthera uncia*, *Pantholops hodgsonii*, *Equus kiang*, and *Bos mutus*.

北京动物园和上海动物园
Beijing Zoo and Shanghai Zoo

1. 北京动物园
1. Beijing Zoo

北京动物园位于北京市西城区西直门外大街，东邻北京展览馆和莫斯科餐厅，占地面积约 86 公顷，水面 8.6 公顷。原名农事实验场、天然博物院、万牲园、西郊公园，是中国开放最早、动物种类最多的动物园，从清光绪三十二年（1906 年）至今已有逾百年的历史。目前饲养展览动物 450 余种 4500 多只；海洋鱼类及海洋生物 500 余种 10000 多尾。每年接待中外游客 600 多万人次。是中国最大的动物园之一，也是一所世界知名的动物园。北京动物园是国家和北京市科普教育基地、全国十佳动物园之首，国家 5A 级旅游景点。

Beijing Zoo is located in Xizhimen Street, Xicheng District, Beijing, adjacent to Beijing Exhibition Center and Moscow Restaurant in the east. It covers a land area of about 86 hectares and water surface of 8.6 hectares. Formerly named Agricultural Experimental Field, Natural Museum, Wansheng Park, and Xijiao Park, it is the first open zoo with the most animal species in China. Dating back to the 32nd year (1906) of Guangxu Emperor in Qing Dynasty, it has a history of more than a century. Currently, it raises and exhibits over 4,500 animals in more than 450 species and over 10,000 marine fish and marine life in 500 species. Receiving more than 6 million Chinese and foreign tourists annually, it is one of the largest zoos in China and also a world-renowned zoo. Beijing Zoo is a national and popular science education base in Beijing, the No. 1 of the top ten national zoos, and a national 5A-class tourist attraction.

2. 上海动物园

2. Shanghai Zoo

上海动物园地处上海市西郊，毗邻虹桥国际机场，原名西郊公园，1980 年改名为上海动物园，是上海市区最佳的生态园林之一。上海动物园内有珍稀动物近 600 种、6000 余只，其中有我国珍贵动物麋鹿、大熊猫、金丝猴、白唇鹿、东北虎、扬子鳄等，还有来自世界各地的长颈鹿、袋鼠、企鹅、河马、海狮、鸵鸟、狮子等。此外，上海动物园内有中国大陆动物园中第一座科学教育馆。

Shanghai Zoo is located in the western suburbs of Shanghai and adjacent to the Hongqiao International Airport. It was formerly known as Xijiao Park and was renamed as Shanghai Zoo in 1980. It is one of the best ecological gardens in Shanghai. There are more than 6,000 heads of rare animals belonging to nearly 600 species in Shanghai Zoo, including precious ones such as *Elaphurus davidianus*, *Ailuropoda melanoleuca*, *Rhinopithecus*, *Cervus albirostris*, *Panthera tigris altaica*, *Alligator sinesis*, as well as *Giraffa camelopardalis*, *Macropodidae*, *Spheniscidae*, *Hippopotamus amphibius*, *Otraiidae*, *Struthio camelus*, *Puma concolor*, and *Panthera leo* from all over the world. In addition, Shanghai Zoo contains the first science education center in mainland of China.

第三节 近些年来我国野生动物保护的一些重大举措

Section Ⅲ Some Major Measures to Protect Wildlife in China in Recent Years

你知道吗?
Do you know?

开展野生动物资源调查是林业主管部门的法定职责，也是科学决策保护措施的基础和评价保护成效的依据。

Conducting surveys on wildlife resources is a statutory responsibility of forestry authorities and the foundation for scientific decision-making and protective measures and basis to evaluate the protection effectiveness.

一、设立实施全国野生动植物保护及自然保护区建设工程

I. Establishing and Implementing National Project on Wildlife Protection and Nature Reserve Construction

为进一步加大野生动植物及其栖息地的保护和管理力度，提高全民野生动植物保护意识，加大对野生动植物保护及自然保护区建设的投入，促进其持续、稳定、健康发展，并在全国生态环境和国民经济建设中发挥更大的作用。1999 年 10 月国家林业局组织有关部门和专家对今后 50 年的全国野生动植物及自然保护区建设进行了全面规划和工程建设安排。2001 年 6 月由国家林业局组织编制的《全国野生动植物保护及自然保护区建设工程总体规划》得到国家计委的正式批准，这标志着中国野生动植物保护和自然保护区建设新纪元的开始。

To further increase the protection and management of wildlife as well as their habitats, enhance the people's awareness of wildlife protection, increase investment in protecting wildlife and nature reserve construction, and promote the sustained, steady and healthy development of wildlife and bring it into full play in the construction of national ecological environment and economy, the State Forestry Administration organized relevant departments and experts to work out comprehensive planning and project arrangements on the construction of national wildlife and nature reserves for the next 50 years in October 1999. In June 2001, the *Master Plan of National Project on Wildlife Protection and Nature Reserve*

Construction prepared by the State Forestry Administration was formally approved by the State Planning Commission, which marked the beginning of the construction of wildlife protection and nature reserve construction in China in the new era.

全国野生动植物保护及自然保护区建设工程是一个面向未来，着眼长远，具有多项战略意义的生态保护工程，也是呼应国际大气候、树立中国良好国际形象的"外交工程"。工程内容包括野生动植物保护、自然保护区建设、湿地保护和基因保存。重点开展物种拯救工程、生态系统保护工程、湿地保护和合理利用示范工程、种质基因保存工程等。

The national project on wildlife protection and nature reserve construction was an ecological protection project that was future-oriented from long-term perspective and with much strategic significance. It was also a "diplomatic project" that echoed the great international climate and establishment of good international image of China. The project work included wildlife protection, construction of nature reserves, wetland protection, and gene conservation. The focus was on species rescue, ecosystem protection, wetland protection and demonstration of rational use, and preservation of germplasm gene.

二、进行全国陆生野生动物资源调查
Ⅱ. Conducting Survey on National Terrestrial Wildlife Resources

继 1995 年开展全国首次陆生野生动物资源调查之后，国家林业局于 2010 年又启动了全国第二次陆生野生动物资源调查。开展陆生野生动物资源调查，掌握全国陆生野生动物资源底数及动态变化情况，不仅是科学决策、检验保护成效的重要依据，也是履行法定职责的要求和夯实保护基础、提高履行国际公约能力、培养调查监测队伍的需要，调查成果将为今后强化野生动物保护监管和相关国际公约履约事务提供科学依据，发挥积极作用。

Following the first national survey of terrestrial wildlife resources in 1995, the State Forestry Administration launched the second survey on national terrestrial wildlife resources in 2010. The aim of conducting survey on terrestrial wildlife resources is to obtain the background data and dynamic changes of them. It is not only an important basis for scientific decision-making and testing the protection effectiveness, but also the requirement to fulfill the statutory responsibility and consolidate the protection foundation, improve the ability to perform international conventions, and train survey and monitoring teams. The survey results will provide scientific basis and play an active role in strengthening the supervision of wildlife protection and fulfilling its obligations under the conventions in the future.

三、设立野生动物产品标识制度
Ⅲ. Establishing Marking System of Wildlife Products

为了加强对我国野生动物资源的保护，国家林业局与国家工商行政管理总局于 2003 年联合发布了《关于对利用野生动物及其产品的生产企业进行清理整顿和开展标记试点工作的通知》，成为我国规范和监管野生动物及其产品市场的一个标志性措施。野生动物经营利用管理专用标识管理制度的核心，是确认野生动物产品来源的合法性。因此，购买野生动物产品，应认准其是否加载有该专用标识。对野生动植物及其产品实行"中国野生动植物管理专用标识制度"，是国家林业局和国家工商行政管理总局经过长期研究、并借鉴国际先进经验的基础上，逐步进行试点实施的。实践证明，标识制度的实行，对于有效调控资源消耗总量，防止非法来源野生动植物及其产品进入市场，规范野生动物产品经营利用行为，提高管理效能，维护企业和消费者合法权益均有突出的成效。此举还得到了国际野生动物保护领域的很高评价。

In order to strengthen the protection of wildlife resources, the State Forestry Administration and the State Administration for Industry and Commerce jointly issued *Circular on Rectifying Manufacturing Enterprises of Wildlife and Their Products and Carrying out Pilot Labeling* in 2003. This has become a symbol measure to regulate and supervise wildlife and their product market in China. The core of special labeling system of wildlife management and use is to identify the legality of sources of wildlife products. Therefore, it was important to identify the special label when buying wildlife products. The "China Special Labeling system for Wildlife Management" has been implemented for wildlife and their products step by step based on a pilot project launched by the State Forestry Administration and the State Administration for Industry and Commerce after a long study and learning from the international advanced experience. Practice has proven that the implementation of labeling systems is effective to effectively control the total consumption of resources, to prevent wildlife and their products coming from illicit origins from entering into the market, to regulate the operation and use of wildlife products, to improve management efficiency, and to safeguard the legitimate rights and interests of enterprises and consumers. This measure has got high evaluation from international wildlife conservation.

"中国野生动物经营利用管理专用标识"由固定的图形文字组合和产品标注两部分组成。固定的图形文字组合包括：雄性梅花鹿头、地球及环绕轨迹，英文字母 CNWM 和"中国野生动物经营利用管理专用标识"字样。鹿头代表以梅花鹿为主的

中国野生动物经营利用管理专用标识
China Mark for Wildlife Management

人工培育资源健康快速发展，地球表示资源保护和发展是全球的共同责任，环绕轨迹表示野生动物资源的可持续发展。产品标注内容包括：物种名称、制品名称和标识代码。"China Mark for Wildlife Management" consists of two parts: fixed combination of text and graphics and product label. The fixed combination of text and graphics includes: a male deer head, the Earth and surrounding tracks, the letters CNWM, and the Chinese characters "China Mark for Wildlife Management". The deer head represents healthy and rapid development of the deer-based artificially bred resources; the Earth represents the common responsibility of resource protection and development around the globe; the surrounding tracks represent sustainable development of wildlife resources. The product label part includes: species name, produce name, and identification code.

研究性学习
Investigative Study

请为我们介绍一下野生动物产品标识制度。
Please introduce the marking system of wildlife products.

拓展阅读
Extended Reading

我国有代表性的自然保护机构
Representative Natural Protection Agencies in China

一、有代表性的自然保护区
Ⅰ. Representative Nature Reserves

1. 黑龙江扎龙国家级自然保护区
1. Zhalong National Nature Reserve in Heilongjiang

黑龙江扎龙国家级自然保护区位于黑龙江省齐齐哈尔市东南部，松嫩平原的西部。地处齐齐哈尔市铁锋区、昂昂溪区、泰来县、富裕县和大庆市杜尔伯特蒙古族自治县、林甸县的交界处。保护区总面积 21 万公顷，其中在齐齐哈尔市行政区域内面积为 9.3 万公顷，在大庆市行政区域内面积为 11.7 万公顷。保护区管理局所在地榆树岗在齐齐哈尔市铁锋区扎龙乡境内。

Zhalong National Nature Reserve is located in the southeast of Qiqihar City, Heilongjiang Province, and on western Songnen Plain. It is at the intersection of Tiefeng District, Angangxi District, Tailai County, and Fuyu County in Qiqihar City and Dorbod Mongol Autonomous County and Lindian County in Daqing City. The nature reserve covers an area of 210,000 hectares, of which 93,000 hectares are administrative area in Qiqihar City and 117,000 hectares are administrative area in Daqing City. Yushugang, where the nature reserve administration is located is in Zhalong Village, Tiefeng District, Qiqihar City.

　　保护区始建于 1979 年，1987 年经国务院批准晋升为国家级自然保护区，1992 年被列入国际重要湿地名录。扎龙自然保护区是松嫩平原保留最完整、生物多样性最丰富的湿地生态系统，也是丹顶鹤等多种珍稀水禽繁殖栖息地。保护区鹤类资源丰富，全世界鹤类有 15 种，我国分布 9 种，扎龙自然保护区有 6 种，其中丹顶鹤种群数量达到 300 只左右。目前，扎龙保护区已经成为全球 16 个湿地保护成功范例之一，亦是研究恢复与重建退化湿地生态系统的天然参照系统。

（陈建伟摄）

俯瞰扎龙
an airview of Zhalong (Credit: Chen Jianwei)

The nature reserve was founded in 1979, was promoted as a national nature reserve by the State Council in 1987, and was included in the Ramsar List of Wetlands of International Importance in 1992. Zhalong Nature Reserve is the wetland ecosystem that is the best preserved with the richest biodiversity on Songnen Plain and is also the breeding site and habitat of many rare waterfowls including *Grus japonensis*. There are rich crane resources in the nature reserve. Of the total 15 crane species in the world, 9 can be found in China, of which 6 are found in Zhalong Nature Reserve, where there are about 300 *Grus japonensis*. Currently, Zhalong Nature Reserve has become one of the world's 16 successful examples of wetland protection and a natural reference system for the study of restoration and rehabilitation of degraded wetland ecosystems.

　　2. 黑龙江珍宝岛湿地国家级自然保护区

2. Zhenbao Island Wetland National Nature Reserve in Heilongjiang

　　黑龙江珍宝岛湿地国家级自然保护区位于虎林市东部，完达山南麓，以乌苏里江为界与俄罗斯联邦隔水相望，是三江平原沼泽湿地集中分布地区。2002 年 4 月，被批准为省级自然保护区；2008 年 1 月，被批准为国家级自然保护区；2011 年 9 月被列入国际重要湿地名录。总面积为 44364 公顷。

Zhenbao Island Wetland National Nature Reserve in Heilongjiang is located in eastern Hulin and the southern foot of Wanda Mountain. It faces the Russian Federation across the Ussuri River and is a concentrated distribution area of marshlands on Sanjiang Plain. In April 2002, it was approved as a provincial nature reserve; in January 2008, it was approved as a national nature reserve; in September 2011, it was included in the Ramsar List of Wetlands of International Importance. It has a total area of 44,364 hectares.

（陈建伟摄）

珍宝岛湿地
Zhenbao Island Wetlands (Credit: Chen Jianwei)

　　保护区主要以沼泽湿地和岛状林为主，大面积的淡水湿地集中连片，是同纬度地区保护原始区域最具有代表性和类型最为典型的沼泽生态系统。湿地大部分保持原始状态，已成为亚洲北部水禽南迁的必经之地和东北亚地区水禽繁殖中心。保护区内容纳了三江平原地区所有的生物物种，其中包括大量濒危的稀有物种，是一个丰富的物质资源基因库。保护区内有珍稀兽类如东北虎、棕熊、黑熊等。有鸟类 169 种，包括丹顶鹤、白枕鹤、东方白鹳、大天鹅、白鹳、白尾海雕、金雕等。鱼类资源丰富，有"三花五罗"等名贵淡水鱼类 40 余种。高等植物 600 余种，分属 130 科，有国家珍稀濒危植物胡桃楸、水曲柳、黄檗、野大豆、五味子、莲、乌苏里狐尾藻等。

The nature reserve is mainly home to marshlands and island forests, with a large area of concentrated freshwater wetlands. It is the most representative and most typical marsh ecosystem in the primitive district at the same latitude. Most of the wetlands remain pristine and have become the path that waterfowls in northern Asia must pass when migrating to the south and the breeding center of waterfowls in Northeast Asia. The nature reserve accommodates all the living species on Sanjiang Plain, including a large number of rare and endangered species, and thus it is a gene pool of rich material resources. The nature reserve has rare mammals such as *Panthera tigris altaica*, *Ursus arctos*, and *Ursus thibetanus*. There are 169 species of birds, including *Grus japonensis*, *Grus vipio*, *Ciconia boyciana*, *Cygnus cygnus*, *Ciconia ciconia*, *Haliaeetus albicilla*, and *Aquila chrysaetos*. It is rich in fish resources and has more than 40 species of rare freshwater fish, including *Siniperca chuatsi*, *Parabramis pekinensis*, *Hemibarbus maculatus*, *Hucho taimen*, *Magalobrame tarminalis*, *Leuciscus*, *Minnow*, and *Nibea albiflora*. There are more than 600 kinds of higher plants belonging to 130 families, including national rare and endangered plants such as *Juglans mandshurica*, *Fraxinus mandshurica*, *Phellodendron amurense*, *Glycine soja*, *Schisandra chinensis*, *Nelumbo nucifera*, and *Myriophyllum ussuriense*.

3. 吉林长白山国家级自然保护区
3. Changbai Mountain National Nature Reserve in Jilin

吉林长白山国家级自然保护区位于吉林省东南部，东南部与朝鲜民主主义人民共和国相毗邻。保护区总面积 196465 公顷。长白山自然保护区始建于 1960 年，是我国建立较早、地位十分重要的自然保护区之一，是以保护生物多样性为主的森林生态系统类型自然保护区。1980 年 1 月，长白山自然保护区被联合国教科文组织纳入"人与生物圈计划"，成为世界生物圈自然保护区网成员，被列为世界自然保留地之一。1986 年 7 月，被国务院批准为"国家级森林和野生动物类型自然保护区"。
Changbai Mountain National Nature Reserve is located in the southeast of Jilin Province, adjacent to the Democratic People's Republic of Korea in southeast. The nature reserve covers a total area of 196,465 hectares. Built in 1960, Changbai Mountain National Nature Reserve is one of the earliest and most important nature reserves in China and a forest ecosystem nature reserve to protect biodiversity. In January 1980, Changbai Mountain National Nature Reserve was included in the UNESCO "Man and the Biosphere Program" to become a member of nature reserve network in the world biosphere and was listed as one of the world's natural reserved areas. In July 1986, it was approved by the State Council as "a national forest and wildlife nature reserve".

长白山自然保护区森林生态系统十分完整，在同纬度带上，其动植物资源十分丰富，是欧亚大陆北半部最具有代表性的典型自然综合体，是世界少有的"物种基因库"，是森林生态系统研究和教学的天然实验室，是进行环境保护和绿色宣传教育的自然博物馆。据统计，长白山自然保护区有野生植物 2806 种，野生动物 1558 种。珍稀动物有紫貂、东北虎、金钱豹、梅花鹿等，珍稀植物有人参、东北红豆杉、长白松等。
Changbai Mountain Nature Reserve has very complete forest ecosystems and rich flora and fauna resources in the same latitude zone. It is the most representative natural complex in the northern half of Eurasia and one of the few "species gene pools" in the world. It is also a natural laboratory for the study and teaching of forest ecosystems and a natural museum for environmental protection and green publicity and education. According to statistics,

Changbai Mountain Nature Reserve has 2,806 species of wild plants and 1,558 species of wild animals. The rare animals include *Martes zibellina*, *Panthera tigris altaica*, *Panthera pardus*, and *Cervus nippon*. The valuable and rare plants include *Panax ginseng*, *Taxus cuspidata*, and *Pinus syluestriformis*.

　　长白山也是松花江、图们江、鸭绿江（以下简称"三江"）的发源地。长白山自然保护区的森林生态系统在涵养水源、保持水土、净化水质和大气、改善区域气候等方面发挥着极其重要的作用，是三江中下游广大地区生态安全的重要绿色屏障。长白山国家级自然保护区是以保护典型的火山地貌景观和复杂的森林生态系统为主要对象，以保存野生动植物种质资源，保护、拯救和扩繁珍稀濒危生物物种，保持生态系统的自然演替过程，保障长白山乃至三江三大水系中下游广大地区的生态安全，保护全人类珍贵的自然遗产为根本目的，集资源保护、科研教学、绿色教育和生态旅游四大功能于一体的综合性自然保护区。

Changbai Mountain is also the origin of Songhua River, Tumen River, and Yalu River (hereinafter referred to as the "Three Rivers"). The forest ecosystem in Changbai Mountain Nature Reserve plays an extremely important role in water conservation, preservation of soil and water, purification of water and air, and improvement of regional climate, and is an important green barrier for the ecological safety in the large middle and lower reaches of the Three Rivers. Changbai Mountain Nature Reserve mainly protects typical volcanic landscapes and complex forest ecosystems, saves germplasm resources of wildlife, protects, rescues and propagates rare and endangered species, maintains the natural evolution process of ecosystems, protects the ecological safety in Changbai Mountain and the large middle and lower reaches of the Three Rivers, and protects the precious natural heritage for all mankind. It is an integrated nature reserve that integrates resource protection, research and teaching, green education, and eco-tourism.

　　4. 内蒙古乌拉特梭梭林蒙古野驴国家级自然保护区

4. Haloxylon Forest and *Equus hemionus* National Nature Reserves in Urat, Inner Mongolia

　　内蒙古乌拉特梭梭林蒙古野驴国家级自然保护区位于内蒙古自治区巴彦淖尔市乌拉特中旗、乌拉特后旗北部，与蒙古国接壤，属荒漠生态系统类型国家级自然保护区。保护区东西纵深 140 千米，南北横跨 22 千米，总面积 131800 公顷。1985 年经内蒙古自治区人民政府批准建立乌拉特后旗努登梭梭林自然保护区，2001 年 6 月，经国务院批准建立乌拉特梭梭林蒙古野驴国家级自然保护区。主要保护对象为该区内分布的原始天然梭梭林和栖息的蒙古野驴、北山羊、鹅喉羚等珍稀野生动物。区内植物区系成分是以干旱地区的种类占主导地位，具有显著的荒漠特点。兽类中属于国家一级保护动物有蒙古野驴、北山羊2种；属于国家二级保护动物有鹅喉羚、盘羊、猞猁、兔狲、荒漠猫5种。保护区鸟类中列入国家一级重点保护种类有大鸨、波斑鸨、金雕3种，列为国家二级重点保护种类有蓑羽鹤、灰鹤、草原雕、鸢、苍鹰、秃鹫、红隼7种。梭梭根部寄生的肉苁蓉具有"沙漠人参"之美称，具有很高的药用价值和经济价值。

Haloxylon Forest and *Equus hemionus* National Nature Reserves in Urat is located in the Middle Banner of Urat and the north of Rear Banner of Urat in Bayannur City, Inner Mongolia Autonomous Region, respectively. They border with Mongolia and are national nature reserves of desert ecosystem. The nature reserves are 140 km depth in the east-west direction and span 22 km in the north-south direction, covering a total area of 131,800 hectares. In 1985, the Norden Haloxylon Forest Nature Reserve was established in the Rear Banner of Urat under the approval of People's Government of Inner Mongolia Autonomous Region; in June 2001, Haloxylon Forest and *Equus hemionus* National Nature Reserve was built in Urat under the approval of the State Council. They mainly protect the primitive natural Haloxylon forest and *Equus hemionus*, *Capra sibirica*, *Gazella subgutturosa*, and other rare wildlife with the forest as habitats. The flora components in the nature reserves are dominated by species in arid areas with obvious desert characteristics. Of the protected beasts, the national first-grade protected animals include *Equus hemionus* and *Capra sibirica*; the national second-grade protected animals include *Gazella subgutturosa*, *Ovis ammon*, *Lynx lynx*, *Otocolobus manul*, and *Felis bieti*. The national first-grade key protected species of birds in the nature reserves include *Otis tarda*, *Chlamydotis macqueenii*, and *Aquila chrysaetos*; the national second-grade protected species include *Anthropoides virgo*, *Grus grus*, *Aquila nipalensis*, *Milvus korschun*, *Accipiter gentilis*, *Aegypius monachus*, and *Falco tinnunculus*. *Cistanche deserticola* in the roots of *Haloxylon ammodendron* is known as "desert ginseng" that has high medicinal value and economic value.

5. 山东黄河三角洲国家级自然保护区

5. Yellow River Delta National Nature Reserve in Shandong

　　山东黄河三角洲国家级自然保护区是以保护黄河口新生湿地生态系统和珍稀濒危鸟类为主体的湿地类型自然保护区，1992年10月由国务院批准建立，同年12月成立自然保护区管理局。总面积1530平方千米，分为南北两个区域，南部区域位于现行黄河入海口，面积1045平方千米；北部区域位于1976年改道后的黄河故道入海口，面积485平方千米。黄河三角洲湿地是世界上土地面积增长最快、国内最大的新生湿地，是中国暖温带最年轻、最广阔、保存最完整的湿地生态系统。同时，黄河携带大量泥沙在这里沉积，使这里成为我国最年轻的土地。区内鸟类众多，共有鸟类298种，其中，有国家一级重点保护鸟类丹顶鹤、东方白鹳等 10 种，有国家二级保护鸟类大天鹅、灰鹤等 49 种。珍稀濒危鸟类逐年增多，每年春、秋候鸟迁徙季节，数百万只鸟类在这里捕食、栖息、翱翔，成为东北亚内陆和环西太平洋鸟类迁徙重要的中转站、越冬栖息地和繁殖地，被誉为"鸟类的国际机场"。区内植物资源丰富，共有植物 400 种，其中野生种子植物 116 种。芦苇、盐地碱蓬、柽柳和罗布麻在自然保护区内广泛分布，是中国沿海最大的新生湿地自然植被区。

Yellow River Delta National Nature Reserve in Shandong is a wetland nature reserve to protect newborn wetland ecosystems and rare and endangered birds in the Yellow River estuary. It was established in October 1992 under the approval of the State Council and founded the Nature Reserves Administration in December the same year. It covers a total area of 1,530 km^2 and is divided into the north and south zones. The south zone is located in the Yellow River estuary with an area of 1,045 km^2; the north zone is located in the Yellow River estuary after diversion in 1976 with an area of 485 km^2. Yellow River Delta wetlands are the fastest growing newborn wetlands in the world and the largest newborn wetlands in China. It is also the youngest, the most extensive, and best preserved wetland ecosystems in the warm temperate zone in China. Meanwhile, the Yellow River carries large amounts of sediments deposited there, making it the youngest land in the Republic. The reserve is home to many birds, including a total of 298 species, of which there are 10 species of national first-grade key protected birds such as *Grus japonensis* and *Ciconia boyciana*. There are 49 species of national second-grade protected birds, including *Cygnus cygnus* and *Grus grus*. Rare and endangered birds increase every year. During the migratory seasons in each spring and autumn, millions of birds prey, settle and soar in the reserve, making it an important stopover site, wintering habitat, and breeding ground of migratory birds in Northeast Asia Inland and Western Pacific Rim and known as "international airport of birds". There are rich plant resources in the reserve, including a total of 400 species, of which there are 116 species of wild seed plants. *Phragmites australis*, *Suaeda salsa*, *Tamarix chinensis*, and *Apocynum venetum* are widely distributed in the nature reserve, making it the largest coastal newborn wetland natural vegetation area in China.

6. 江西鄱阳湖国家级自然保护区
6. Poyang Lake National Nature Reserve in Jiangxi

江西鄱阳湖国家级自然保护区成立于 1983 年，1988 年晋升为国家级自然保护区，主要职能是保护鄱阳湖以白鹤为代表的珍稀候鸟和湿地生态环境。保护区位于鄱阳湖的西北角，地跨新建、永修和星子 3 县，管辖有沙湖、大汊湖、蚌湖、朱市湖、梅西湖、象湖、大湖池、常湖池、中湖池 9 个湖泊，总面积为 22400 公顷。

Poyang Lake National Nature Reserve in Jiangxi was founded in 1983 and was promoted to be a national nature reserve in 1988. Its main function is to protect rare migratory birds represented by white cranes and wetland ecological environment in Poyang Lake. The nature reserve is located in the northwest corner of the Poyang Lake and spans across three counties of Xinjian, Yongxiu, and Xingzi. Under its jurisdiction are 9 lakes of Shahu Lake, Dacha Lake, Banghu Lake, Zhushi Lake, Meixi Lake, Xianghu Lake, Dahuchi Lake, Changhuchi Lake, and Zhonghuchi Lake, with a total area of 22,400 hectares.

保护区内湿地生态系统结构完整，生物资源丰富。据初步统计，有鸟类 310 种、贝类 40 种、兽类 45 种、浮游动物 46 种、爬行类 48 种、浮游植物 50 种、鱼类 136 种、昆虫类 227 种、高等植物 476 种。鸟类中属于国家一级保护鸟类 10 种：白鹤、白头鹤、东方白鹳、黑鹳、中华秋沙鸭、金雕、乌雕、白肩雕、白尾海雕、大鸨；国家二级保护鸟类 41 种。每年到鄱阳湖越冬的候鸟数量多达 60 万～70 万只。越冬白鹤最高数量达 4000 只，占全球 98% 以上。全世界 80% 以上的东方白鹳、70% 以上的白枕鹤在鄱阳湖保护区内越冬。这里是世界上最大的鸿雁种群越冬地（数量达 6 万多只），也是中国最大的小天鹅种群越冬地（最高数量达 7 万只），同时也是大量珍稀候鸟的重要迁徙通道和停歇地，有 10 余种南北半球间迁徙的鸻鹬类在鄱阳湖补充食物，其数量也达到了全球数量的 1% 以上，是候鸟迁徙的重要位点。

The nature reserve has complete wetland ecosystem structures and rich biological resources. According to preliminary statistics, there are 310 species of birds, 40 species of shellfish, 45 species of beasts, 46 species of zooplankton, 48 species of reptiles, 50 species of phytoplankton, 136 species of fish, 227 species of insects, and 476 species of higher plants in the nature reserve. There are 10 species of national first-grade protected birds: *Grus leucogeranus*, *Grus monacha*, *Ciconia boyciana*, *Ciconia nigra*, *Mergus squamatus*, *Aquila chrysaetos*, *Aquila clanga*, *Aquila heliaca*, *Haliaeetus albcilla*, and *Otis tarda*; there are 41 species of national second-grade protected birds. Each year, 600,000 to 700,000 migratory birds spend the winter in Poyang Lake. The maximum number of wintering *Grus leucogeranus* is more than 4,000, accounting for more than 98% of the world. Over 80% of *Ciconia boyciana* and over 70% of *Grus vipio* in the world spend the winter in the Poyang Lake Nature Reserve. This is the largest wintering site for *Anser cygnoides* (more than 60,000) in the world and for *Cygnus columbianus* (more than 70,000) in China. It is also an important migratory path and stopover site of a large number of rare migratory birds. More than 10 species of shorebirds migrating between northern and southern hemispheres replenish food in Poyang Lake, accounting for more than 1% of the total number in the world, making the nature reserve an important site for the migration of birds.

7. 福建梅花山国家级自然保护区

7. Meihua Mountain National Nature Reserve in Fujian

福建梅花山国家级自然保护区于 1985 年 4 月经福建省人民政府批准建立，1988 年 5 月经国务院批准列为国家级森林和野生动物类型自然保护区。保护区地处福建西南部，是武夷山脉南段与博平岭之间的玳瑁山的主体部分，为上杭、连城、龙岩三县（市）交界地带。保护区总面积为 22168.5 公顷。梅花山自然保护区地处中亚热带南缘，气候具有从中亚热带向南亚热带过渡的特点，是福建三大水系闽江、汀江、九龙江的发源地。保护区内的珍稀野生动物有华南虎、金钱豹、云豹、金猫、水鹿、梅花鹿等，还有金斑啄凤蝶、詹彩臂金龟等珍稀昆虫。

Meihua Mountain National Nature Reserve in Fujian was founded under the approval of People's Government of Fujian Province in April 1985 and was listed as a national forest and wildlife nature reserve under the approval of the State Council in May 1988. Located in the southwest of Fujian Province, the nature reserve is the main part of Daimao Mountain between the southern section of Wuyi Mountain and Bopingling and is in the border area of Shanghang, Liancheng, and Longyan counties. It covers a total area of 22,168.5 hectares. Meihua Mountain Nature Reserve is located in the southern edge of the mid-subtropical zone, with a climate transition from mid-subtropical characteristics to south subtropical ones. It is the birthplace of the three water systems in Fujian: Minjiang River, Tingjiang River, and Jiulong River. The rare wildlife in the nature reserve includes *Panthera trigris amoyensis*, *Panthera pardus*, *Neofelis nebulosa*, *Catopuma temminckii*, *Rusa unicolor*, and *Cervus nippon*, as well as rare insects like *Teinopalpus aureus* and *Cheirotonus jansoni*.

8. 陕西佛坪国家级自然保护区

8. Foping National Nature Reserve in Shaanxi

陕西佛坪国家级自然保护区是 1978 年经国务院批准建立的以保护大熊猫及其栖息地为主的森林和野生动物类型国家级自然保护区，地处秦岭中段主脊南侧，总面积 29240 公顷，居于秦岭自然保护区群的中心位置。由于地理位置独特，区内具有典型的北亚热带与暖温带交汇的山地森林生态系统以及丰富多样的生物资源，分布有国家重点保护动物 45 种，其中大熊猫、朱鹮、川金丝猴、羚牛等一级保护动物 8 种；黑熊、红腹锦鸡等二级保护动物 38 种。有高等植物 1769 种，其中红豆杉、独叶草等国家重点保护植物 64 种。大熊猫的分布密度居全国前列，生物学家称这里是"生物资源的宝库，野生动物的天堂，科学研究的理想场所"。

Foping National Nature Reserve in Shaanxi is a forest and wildlife national nature reserve founded in 1978 under the approval of the State Council to protect the *Ailuropoda melanoleuca* and its habitats. It is located in the south of the main ridge of Qinling Mountains, with a total area of 29,240 hectares. It is the center of the cluster of Qinling Nature Reserves. Due to the unique geographical location, the reserve has typical mountain forest ecosystems at the intersection of northern subtropical zone and warm temperate zone and rich biodiversity. There are 45 species of national key protection animals in the reserve, including 8 national first-grade protected animals such as *Ailuropoda melanoleuca*, *Nipponia nippon*, *Rhinopithecus roxellana*, and *Budorcas taxicolor*; there are 38 species of national second-grade protected animals including *Ursus thibetanus* and *Chrysolophus pictus*. There are 1,769 species of higher plants, including 64 species of national key protected plants like *Taxus chinensis* and *Kingdonia uniflora*. The distribution density of *Ailuropoda melanoleuca* ranks the first in the country. Biologists call it as the "treasure of biological resources, paradise of wildlife, and ideal place for scientific research".

9. 四川卧龙国家级自然保护区
9. Wolong National Nature Reserve in Sichuan

卧龙自然保护区位于四川省阿坝藏族、羌族自治州汶川县西南部，邛崃山脉东南坡，距四川省会成都 130 千米，交通便利。保护区始建于 1963 年，面积 20 万公顷，是我国最早建立的综合性国家级保护区之一。卧龙自然保护区以"熊猫之乡""宝贵的生物基因库""天然动植物园"享誉中外，有着丰富的动植物资源和矿产资源。区内共分布着 100 多只大熊猫。被列为国家级重点保护的其他珍稀濒危动物金丝猴、羚牛等共有 56 种，其中属于国家一级重点保护的野生动物共有 12 种，二级保护动物 44 种。据已采集的植物标本统计，区内植物有近 4000 种。被列为国家级保护的珍贵濒危植物达 24 种，其中一级保护植物有珙桐、连香树、水青树，二级保护植物 9 种，三级保护植物 13 种。保护区内还有丰富的水能蕴藏量。

Wolong National Nature Reserve in Sichuan is located in the southwest of Wenchuan County of Aba Tibetan and Qiang Autonomous Prefecture, Sichuan Province, and in the southeast slope of Qionglai Mountain Range, 130 km from the provincial capital Chengdu. The transportation there is convenient. The nature reserve was founded in 1963, covering an area of 200,000 hectares. It is one of the earliest comprehensive national nature reserves. Wolong Nature Reserve is known as "home of pandas", "valuable biological gene bank", and "natural zoo and botanical garden" in the world. It has rich flora and fauna resources and mineral resources. More than 100 *Ailuropoda melanoleuca* are distributed in the reserve. There are also other 56 rare and endangered animal species that are national key protected targets in the nature reserve, including *Rhinopithecus* and *Budorcas taxicolor*. Of these animals, 12 species are national first-grade key protected wildlife and 44 species are national second-grade protected targets. According to statistics of the collected plant specimens, there are nearly 4,000 species of plants in the reserve, and 24 are listed as national protected rare and endangered plants. The national first-grade protected plants include *Davidia involucrata*, *Cercidiphyllum japonicum*, and *Tetracentron sinense Oliv*, while there are 9 species of national second-grade protected plants and 13 species of national third-grade protected plants. There is also rich hydroenergy potential in the reserve.

卧龙自然保护区地理条件独特、地貌类型复杂，风景秀丽、景型多样、气候宜人，集山、水、林、洞、险、峻、奇、秀于一体，还有浓郁的藏、羌民族文化。区内建有相当规模的大熊猫、小熊猫、金丝猴等国家保护动物繁殖场，圈养大熊猫总数达到80余只，占世界圈养种群的60%；有世界著名的"五一棚"大熊猫野外观测站；有国内迄今为止以单一生物物种为主建立的博物馆——大熊猫博物馆。

Wolong Nature Reserve has unique geographical conditions and complex topography. The beautiful scenery, diverse landscape types, and pleasant climate there make it a complex site that integrates mountain, water, forest, and cave giving impression that it is dangerous, steep, grotesque, and beautiful. The reserve is also characterized by strong Tibetan and Qiang ethnic cultures. There are considerable sizes of breeding farms for national protected animals such as *Ailuropoda melanoleuca*, *Ailurus fulgens*, and *Rhinopithecus*. There are more than 80 *Ailuropoda melanoleuca* in captivity, accounting for 60% of the captive population in the world. There are the world famous "Wuyipeng", wild panda observatory and Giant Panda Museum, which is only museum that built for one single species in the country.

10. 湖南壶瓶山国家级自然保护区
10. Huping Mountain National Nature Reserve in Hunan

湖南壶瓶山国家级自然保护区地处湖南省石门县境内，总面积66568公顷。该区于1982年经湖南省人民政府批准成立省级自然保护区，1994年经国务院批准晋升为国家级自然保护区，是以保护华南虎等濒危动物物种及其栖息地和珙桐等珍稀植物物种及群落为主的森林和野生动植物类型自然保护区。该区地处云贵高原向东部低山丘陵的过渡地带，区内保存有大量的古老珍稀濒危物种，被国外专家学者誉为"华中地区弥足珍贵的物种基因库"。

Huping Mountain National Nature Reserve in Hunan is located in Shimen County, Hunan Province, with a total area of 66,568 hectares. The reserve is a provincial nature reserve built in 1982 under the approval of the People's Government of Hunan Province and was promoted in 1994 by the State Council as a national nature reserve. It is a forest and wildlife nature reserve that protects endangered animal species like *Panthera trigris amoyensis* and their habitats as well as rare plant species like *Davidia involucrata* and biomes. The reserve is located in the transitional zone from Yunnan-Guizhou Plateau to the eastern low hills. There are large numbers of ancient rare and endangered species in the reserve, and it is described by foreign experts and scholars as "precious species gene pool in Central China".

11. 海南五指山国家级自然保护区
11. Wuzhi Mountain National Nature Reserve in Hainan

海南五指山国家级自然保护区建于 1985 年，2003 年晋升为国家级自然保护区。该保护区地处海南岛中部，位于以五指山顶峰为中心的广大山区，横跨海南省五指山市和琼中县，与保亭县接壤。总面积 13435.9 公顷。是我国以保护原始热带雨林生态系统、珍稀动植物资源及栖息地为主的森林生态系统类型自然保护区，是海南岛原始林面积最大、海拔高差最大、热带植被类型最多、植被垂直带谱最完整、雨林群落最为典型的自然保护区之一，也是生物多样性最为丰富的地区，生态地位十分重要，在我国和全球生物多样性保护中具有重大价值。五指山是海南岛的象征，也是中国名山之一，是海南最高峰，海拔 1867 米。五指山有五峰，形如五指，故得名。五指山与南美洲的亚马孙河流域、印度尼西亚的热带雨林并成为全球保存最完好的三块热带雨林，被誉为海南岛之"肺"。五指山遍布热带原始森林，是海南主要河流昌化江、万泉河的发源地，不仅自然风光优美，且极具神秘色彩。森林中有野生维管植物种类 2146 种，野生动物 289 种，是一个生物多样性极为丰富的宝库。

Wuzhi Mountain National Nature Reserve in Hainan was founded in 1985 and was promoted as a national nature reserve in 2003. The reserve is located in central Hainan and in the broad mountainous area with the peak of Wuzhi Mountain as the center. It spans across Wuzhishan City and Qiongzhong County and borders with Baoting County in Hainan. With a total area of 13,435.9 hectares, it is a nature reserve of forest ecosystem to protect primitive tropical rainforest ecosystem and rare animal and plant resources, as well as their habitats. It is a nature reserve with one of the largest virgin forests, the largest elevation differences, the most tropical vegetation varieties, the most complete vegetation vertical zonation, and the most typical rainforest community in Hainan Island. It is also the area with the richest biodiversity in Hainan Island and occupies very important ecological position. It is of great value in the national and global biodiversity conservation. Wuzhi Mountain is the symbol of Hainan Island and is one of the most famous mountains in China. It is the highest peak in Hainan, with an elevation of 1,867 m. Wuzhi Mountain has five peaks looking like five fingers and thus earns the name "Wuzhi", which means five fingers in Chinese. Wuzhi Mountain, Amazon River basin in South America, and the tropical rainforest in Indonesia are the most well-preserved tropical rainforests in the world. Wuzhi Mountain is regarded as the "lung" of Hainan Island. It is surrounded by tropical forests and the birthplace of major rivers in

Hainan, including Changhua River and Wanquan River. It is not only beautiful with natural scenery, but also very mysterious. With 2,146 species of wild vascular plants and 289 species of wild animals, it is a treasure with rich biodiversity.

12. 云南西双版纳国家级自然保护区
12. Xishuangbanna National Nature Reserve in Yunnan

　　云南西双版纳自然保护区始建于 1958 年，1986 年经国务院批准为国家级自然保护区。保护区在西双版纳傣族自治州境内，由勐腊、尚勇、勐仑、勐养、曼搞等互不相连的 5 片组成，总面积为 241776 公顷。该保护区以保护热带雨林、热带季雨林和南亚热带季风常绿阔叶林森林生态系统和珍稀动植物物种资源为主。已鉴定的高等植物约 3890 种，其中国家重点保护植物有望天树、版纳青梅、苏铁、藤枣、黑黄檀、滇南风吹楠、千果榄仁、四数木、合果木、大叶木兰、红椿、粗枝崖摩、桫椤等 53 种。珍稀动物有亚洲象、印度支那虎、金钱豹、野牛、懒猴、白颊长臂猿、 黑长臂猿、小熊猫、金猫、菲氏叶猴、穿山甲、犀鸟、绿孔雀、白腹黑啄木鸟等。

Xishuangbanna National Nature Reserve in Yunnan was founded in 1958 and was approved as a national nature reserve by the State Council in 1986. The nature reserve is located in the Xishuangbanna Dai Autonomous Prefecture, and is composed of 5 non-contiguous land of Mongla, Shangyong, Menglun, Mengyang, and Mangao, with a total area of 241,776 hectares. The nature reserve is dominated by ecosystems of tropical rainforest, tropical monsoon forest and southern subtropical monsoon evergreen broad-leaved forest, as well as rare plant and animal species resources. There are about 3,890 species of identified higher plants there, including 53 species of national key protected plants such as *Parashorea chinensis, Vatica xishuangbannaensis, Cycas revoluta, Eleutharrhena macrocarpa, Dalbergia fusca, Horsfieldia tetratepala, Terminalia myriocarpa, Tetrameles nudiflora, Paramichelia baillonii, Magnolia henryi, Toona ciliate, Amoora dasyclada*, and *Cyathea spinulosa*. The rare animals include *Elephas maximus, Panthera tigris corbetti, Panthera pardus, Bos gaurus, Nycticebus coucang, Nomascus leucogenys, Nomascus concolor, Ailurus fulgens, Catopuma temminckii, Trachypithecus phayrei, Manis, Hornbill, Pavo muticus*, and *Dryocopus javensis*.

13. 新疆阿尔金山国家级自然保护区
13. Altun Mountains National Nature Reserve in Xinjiang

　　新疆阿尔金山国家级自然保护区位于新疆维吾尔自治区若羌县南部阿尔金山以南，东至新疆、青海省界，南至新疆、西藏间的昆仑山，西至且末县东南角，北沿祁漫塔格山脊向东向西延伸。东西长 360 千米，南北宽 190 千米，总面积为 44940 平方千米。阿尔金山自然保护区内高山环绕，最高的慕士塔格峰海拔 6973 米。现代冰川、高原湖泊和高原沙漠与雪豹、西藏野驴、藏羚、野牦牛、野骆驼、盘羊、鹅喉羚及金雕、白肩雕、玉带海雕、黑颈鹤、藏雪鸡等珍禽异兽，连同 241 种野生植物，蔚为高原奇观。

Altun Mountains National Nature Reserve in Xinjiang is located to the south of Altun Mountains in the south of Ruoqiang County in Xinjiang Uygur Autonomous Region. It spans to the borders of Xinjiang and Qinghai Province in the east, Kunlun Mountains between Xinjiang and Tibet in the south, the southeast corner of Qiemo County in the west, and extending along the ridge of Qimantag Mountains from east to west in the north. It is 360 km long from east to west and 190 km wide from north to south, with a total area of 44,940 km². Altun Mountains Nature Reserve is surrounded by mountains. The peak, Muztagh Ata, is 6,973 m above sea level. Modern glaciers, plateau lakes and plateau deserts, together with rare wildlife like *Panthera uncia*, *Equus kiang*, *Pantholops hodgsoni*, *Bos mutus*, *Camelus ferus*, *Ovis ammon*, *Gazella subgutturosa*, and *Aquila chrysaetos*, *Aquila heliaca*, *Haliaeetus leucoryphus*, *Grus nigricollis*, and *Tetraogallus tibetanus*, as well as 241 species of wild plants, form a spectacular plateau landscape.

14. 青海湖国家级自然保护区
14. Qinghai Lake National Nature Reserve

青海省青海湖国家级自然保护区位于青藏高原东北部，祁连山系南麓，总面积为 4952 平方千米。青海湖自然保护区是以保护青海湖湿地以及鸟类资源及其栖息地为宗旨，集资源保护、科学研究、生态旅游于一体的自然保护区。青海湖是中国最大的内陆湖泊，中国最大的咸水湖。青海湖是维系青藏高原东北部生态安全的重要水体，是阻挡西部荒漠化向东蔓延的天然屏障，是青藏高原生物多样性最丰富的宝库，是水禽的集中栖息地和繁殖育雏场所，也是极度濒危动物普氏原羚的唯一栖息地。成为研究鸟类迁徙规律、研究高原动物食物链、生态环境、生物多样性的宝库，成为高原生物重要基因库。

Qinghai Lake National Nature Reserve in Qinghai Province is located in the northeastern part of the Tibetan Plateau and the southern foot of Qilian Mountains, with a total area of 4,952 km². Qinghai Lake Nature Reserve is to protect wetlands and bird resources as well as their habitats in Qinghai Lake and integrates resource protection, scientific research, and eco-tourism as a whole. Qinghai Lake is the largest inland lake and largest saltwater lake in China. It is the main water body to maintain the ecological safety in the northeastern part of the Tibetan Plateau, a natural barrier to prevent the west desertification from spreading eastward, the treasure of richest biodiversity on the Tibetan Plateau, the concentrated habitat and breeding ground of waterfowls, and the only habitat for the critically endangered *Procapra przewalskii*. It is an ideal place to study migration patterns of birds, the food chain of plateau animals, the ecological environment, and biodiversity, and an important gene pool of plateau creatures.

15. 西藏珠穆朗玛峰国家级自然保护区
15. Mount Everest National Nature Reserve in Tibet

珠穆朗玛峰自然保护区于 1988 年成立，1994 年晋升为国家级自然保护区。保护区位于我国西藏自治区与尼泊尔王国交界处，地处西藏自治区日喀则市的定日县、聂拉木县、吉隆县和定结县四县交界，总面积约 33810 平方千米。主要保护对象为高山、高原生态系统。该保护区内有世界最高峰——珠穆朗玛峰和其他四座海拔 8000 米以上的山峰。保护区内生态系统类型多样，基本保持原貌，生物资源丰富，珍稀濒危物种、新种及特有种较多。保护区内国家一类保护动物有长尾叶猴、熊猴、喜马拉雅塔尔羊、金钱豹、西藏野驴、雪豹、红胸角雉、黑颈鹤；国家二类保护动物有小熊猫、黑熊、藏雪鸡、岩羊等；国家重点保护植物有长蕊木兰、西藏延龄草、天麻、锡金海棠、参三七、长叶云杉、长叶松等。其中引人注目的是属中亚地区特有种的雪豹，已被列为珠峰自然保护区标志动物。

(陈建伟摄)
珠穆朗玛峰晨曦
dawn at Mount Everest(Credit: Chen Jianwei)

The Mount Everest National Nature Reserve was founded in 1988 and was promoted as a national nature reserve in 1994. The nature reserve is located in the boundary of the Tibet Autonomous Region and the Kingdom of Nepal and in the intersection of Tingri County, Nyalam County, Gyirong County, and Dinggye County in Shigatse City in Tibet Autonomous Region, with a total area of about 33,810 km². The main protection targets are high mountain and plateau ecosystems. Located in the nature reserve is the world's peak—Mount Everest, as well as other four peaks over 8,000 m above sea level. There are diverse types of ecosystems in the nature reserve, and they basically remain unchanged, with rich biological resources and many rare and endangered species, as well as new and endemic species. The national first-grade protected animals in the nature reserve include *Semnopithecus entellus*, *Macaca assamensis*, *Hemitragus jemlahicus*, *Panthera pardus*, *Equus kiang*, *Panthera uncia*, *Tragopan temminckii*, and *Grus nigricollis*; the national second-grade protected animals include *Ailurus fulgens*, *Ursus thibetanus*, *Tetraogallus tibetanus*, and *Pseudois nayaur*; the national key protected plants include

Alcimandra cathcardii, *Trillium govanianum*, *Gastrodia elata*, *Malus sikkimensis*, *Radix notoginseng*, *Picea smithiana*, and *Pinus palustris*. Among them, the striking one is *Panthera uncia*, an endemic species in Central Asia that has been listed as a symbol animal in the Mount Everest Nature Reserve.

二、有代表性的国家森林公园
Ⅱ. Representative National Forest Parks

1. 湖南张家界国家森林公园
1. Zhangjiajie National Forest Park in Hunan

张家界国家森林公园建于 1982 年，位于湖南省张家界市，是我国第一个国家森林公园。公园以独特的石英砂峰林地貌著称，集"雄、奇、幽、野、秀"为一体，是"缩小的仙境，扩大的盆景"。公园已开辟黄石寨、金鞭溪、鹞子寨、袁家界等精品游览线，130 多处精华景点。公园不仅自然景观奇特，而且动植物资源异常丰富。有木本植物 93 科 517 种，观赏植物 720 种，鸟类 13 科 41 种，兽类 28 种，有"天然植物园""动物王国"之称。

Zhangjiajie National Forest Park was founded in 1982 and is located in Zhangjiajie City, Hunan Province. It is the first national forest park in China. The park is known for its unique peak forest of quartz sand, giving an impression that it is magnificent, grotesque, quiet, beautiful and wild, and can be described as a "mini wonderland but macro potted landscape". The park has opened tour routes of Huangshizhai, Jinbianxi, Yaozizhai, and Yuanjiajie and provides over 130 attractions. The park has not only unique natural landscape but also exceptionally rich flora and fauna resources. There are 517 species of woody plants belonging to 93 families, 720 species of ornamental plants, 41 species of birds belonging to 13 families, and 28 species of beasts in the park. It is known as "natural botanical garden"and "animal kingdom".

张家界国家森林公园以峰称奇，以谷显幽，以林见秀，3000 座石峰拔地而坡，形态各异，峰林间峡谷幽深，溪流潺潺。春天山花烂漫，花香扑鼻；夏天凉风习习，最宜避暑；秋日红叶遍山，山果挂枝；冬天银装素裹，满山雪白。公园一年四季气候宜人，景色各异，是人们理想的旅游、度假、休闲目的地。

Zhangjiajie National Forest Park is known for its grotesque peaks, quiet valleys, and beautiful forests. More than 3,000 stone peaks with different shapes rise from the ground, and the valleys between the peaks and forests are deep with gurgling streams. In spring, flowers are blooming and fragrant; in summer, the desirable breeze provides the best summer resort; in autumn, the mountains are covered with red leaves and fruits; in winter, the mountains are clad in silvery white. The park enjoys pleasant climates and varied scenery all the year round, serving as an ideal destination for traveling, vacation, and leisure.

2. 黑龙江五大连池国家森林公园
2. Wudalianchi National Forest Park in Heilongjiang

黑龙江五大连池国家森林公园位于五大连池风景名胜区，地处黑龙江省北部，毗邻五大连池市（原德都县）、讷河市、嫩江县、孙吴县和北安市。周围共 14 座火山锥，800 平方千米的熔岩台地，千姿百态的喷气锥碟、终年冰封的熔岩隧道，共同书写着惊心动魄的地质变迁史，生动地展示了地球地壳形成进程。火山岩中的地下水运动形成了 127 眼含有丰富化学成分的天然冷矿泉，具有极高的医疗保健作用，使五大连池成为中国著名的矿泉城和中国矿泉水之乡。五大连池不仅展示了火山爆发的历史长卷，还展示了火山爆发后，生命对熔岩的占领和演变过程。五大连池内植物有 618 种，野生动物 397 种，与同纬度地区相比，动植物种类十分丰富，成为生态演变过程的主要见证，展示了大自然顽强的生命力，是世界上研究物种适应和生物群落演化的最佳地区。

Wudalianchi National Forest Park in Heilongjiang is located in the scenic spot of Wudalianchi in the north of Heilongjiang Province, adjacent to Wudalianchi City (formerly Dedu County), Nehe City, Nenjiang County, Sunwu County and Bei'an City. It is surrounded by a total of 14 volcanic cones and 800 km^2 of lava plateau. The oddly-shaped fumaroles and year-round frozen lava tunnels together record the thrilling geological history and vividly show the crust formation process of the Earth. The groundwater movement under the volcanic rocks developed 127 natural cold mineral springs with rich chemical composition and high health care value, making Wudalianchi the famous home of mineral spring and mineral water in China. Wudalianchi not only unfolds the long history scroll of volcanic eruption, but also demonstrates the occupation and evolution of life on the lava after the volcanic eruptions. There are 618 species of plants and 397 species of wild animals within Wudalianchi. Compared with areas at the same latitude, it is very rich in flora and fauna species and is a major witness of ecological evolution. It shows the tenacious vitality of nature and is the best region to study species adaptation and evolution of biomes in the world.

3. 北京八达岭国家森林公园
3. Badaling National Forest Park in Beijing

北京八达岭国家森林公园位于万里长城八达岭和居庸关之间，总面积 29.33 平方千米（4.4 万亩），最高峰海拔 1238 米，分布植物 539 种、动物 158 种、林木绿化率达到 96%，为中国首家通过 FSC 国际认证的生态公益林区。公园主要景区有红叶岭风景区、青龙谷风景区、丁香谷风景区、石峡风景区。

Badaling National Forest Park in Beijing is located between Badaling of the Great Wall and Juyong Pass, with a total area of 29.33km^2(44,000 mu) and the highest peak of 1,238 m above sea level. There are 539 kinds of plants and 158 kinds of animals distributed there, with a greening rate of 96%. It is the first ecological public-welfare forest certified by FSC in China. The park has the scenic spots of Red Ridge, Qinglong Valley, Dingxiang Valley, and Shixia Valley.

红叶辉映残长城和望龙系列景点是公园的最佳景观，其他还有暴马丁香、杏花、梨花等高价值独特景观资源。詹天佑修建的中华第一条铁路 —— "人"字形铁路位于公园境内。

Red leaves covering the Great Wall and the scenic spots of Wanglong series are best attractions in the park. In addition, there are high-value unique landscape resources like *Syringa reticulata*, *Prunus armeniaca*, and *Pyrus* ssp. The first railway in China, a herringboned railway built by Zhan Tianyou, is located in the park.

因海拔高（平均 750 米）、森林茂盛和古长城隔挡作用，公园常年气温比市区低 5℃，负氧离子含量极丰富，是首都春天离开最晚、夏日最清凉、秋彩来临最早且最艳、冬雪最富意境的地方。

Due to the high altitude (average 750 m), lush forests and the barrier of ancient Great Wall, the year-round temperature in the park is 5 ℃ lower than that in urban areas. It has rich negative oxygen ions and is the place to have the longest spring, the coolest summer, the earliest autumn, and the most colorful and artistic winter.

4. 湖北神农架国家森林公园
4. Shennongjia National Forest Park in Hubei

湖北神农架国家森林公园位于湖北省西北部，由房县、兴山、巴东三县边缘地带组成，面积 3250 平方千米，林地占 85% 以上，森林覆盖率 69.5%，区内居住着汉、土家、回等民族，人口近 8 万。神农架最高峰神农顶海拔 3105.4 米，最低处海拔 398 米，平均海拔 1700 米，3000 米以上的山峰有 6 座，被誉为"华中屋脊"。

Shennongjia National Forest Park in Hubei is located in the northwest of Hubei Province and is composed of the edges of Fangxian County, Xingshan County, and Badong County, with an area of 3,250 km^2. The forest accounts for more than 85% of the land and the forest coverage rate is 69.5%. The area is inhabited by the Han, Tujia and Hui nationalities, with a population of nearly 80,000. Shennong Peak, the highest part of Shennongjia, has an elevation of 3,105.4 m, while the lowest elevation is 398 m. The average altitude is 1,700 m. There are 6 peaks over 3,000 m. The park is known as the "roof of Central China".

神农架素有科学迷宫之称，除举世闻名的"野人"之谜外，还有神奇的白化动物，吸引着科学考察人员和海内外游客。神农架是我国国家级风景名胜区，主要景点有风景垭、板壁岩、大九湖、神农顶、植物园、炎帝祭坛、千年古杉、香溪源、天门垭、燕子垭、植物标本馆、红坪画廊、古犀牛洞等。

Shennongjia is known as a science maze. In addition to the world-famous mystery of "savages", there are amazing albino animals that attract scientific investigators and tourists from home and abroad. Shennongjia is a national top scenic spot and has the main attractions including Fengjing Pass, Banbi Rock, Dajiu Lake, Shennong Peak, Botanical Garden, Altar of Emperor Yan, Millennium Ancient Fir, Xiangxi River Source, Tianmen Pass, Swallow Pass, Herbarium, Hongping Gallery, and Ancient Rhino Hole.

5. 四川九寨国家森林公园
5. Jiuzhai National Forest Park in Sichuan

四川九寨国家森林公园建于 1995 年。公园位于四川省阿坝藏族羌族自治州九寨沟县境内，地处世界自然遗产九寨沟与黄龙之间，东距九寨沟 13 千米，南离黄龙 65 千米，距九寨—黄龙国际旅游机场 20 千米，位于"大九寨"国际旅游区的核心区域。公园面积 37000 公顷，实际经营面积 46000 公顷，包括神仙池（嫩恩桑措）和甘海子两大旅游区。

Jiuzhai National Forest Park in Sichuan was built in 1995. The park is located in Jiuzhaigou County, Autonomous Prefecture of Tibetan and Qiang Nationalities, Aba, Sichuan. It is situated between the world natural heritage Jiuzhaigou Valley and Huanglong. It is 13 km from Jiuzhaigou Valley in the east, 65 km from Huanglong in the south, and 20 km from Jiuzhaigou – Huanglong International Tourism Airport. It is the core area of "Great Jiuzhai" international tourism zone. The park covers an area of 37,000 hectares and the actual operating area of 46,000 hectares, including two attractions of Goddess Lake (Nen'ensangcuo) and Ganhaizi.

九寨国家森林公园位于我国亚热带秦巴湿润区和青藏高原波密—川西湿润区过渡地带。公园内有着丰富的景观资源：森林、水体、地貌等自然景观和民风民俗、神奇传说等人文景观都独具特色。园内地貌类型奇特，植物种类繁多，奇花异草云集，据初步调查有高等植物 1200 余种，森林覆盖率达 70% 以上，珍稀植物有：红豆杉、麦吊云杉、四川红杉、大果青扦、岷江柏木、领春木、羽叶丁香、连香树、水青树、华榛、独叶草、星叶草、天麻、冬虫夏草、雪莲、大叶柳、桃儿七、八角莲等。茂密、原始、良好的森林植被又为野生动物提供了良好的生存繁衍的条件。珍稀动物有大熊猫、羚牛、川金丝猴、毛冠鹿、水獭等。

Jiuzhai National Forest Park is located in the transitional zone between Qinba humid subtropical zone and Bomi‑Chuanxi humid zone of Qinghai-Tibet Plateau. The park has a wealth of unique landscape resources: natural landscapes such as forests, water bodies, and geographical forms, as well as cultural landscapes like folk customs and magical legends. The park has peculiar landforms and a variety of special plants. According to a preliminary survey, it is home to more than 1,200 species of higher plants and the forest coverage rate is over 70%. The rare plants in the park include *Taxus chinensis*, *Picea brachytyla*, *Larix mastersiana*, *Picea neoveitchii*, *Cupressus chengiana*, *Euptelea pleiosperma*, *Syringa pinnatifolia*, *Cercidiphyllum japonicum*, *Tetracentron sinense*, *Corylus chinensis*, *Kingdonia uniflora*, *Circaeaster agrestis*, *Gastrodia elata*, *Cordyceps sinensis*, *Saussurea involucrate*, *Salix magnifica*, *Himalayan mayapple*, and *Dysosma versipellis*. Dense, primitive and good forest vegetation provides good survival and breeding conditions for wildlife. The rare animals include *Ailuropoda meianoieuca*, *Budorcas taxicolor*, *Rhinopithecus roxellana*, *Elaphodus cephalophus*, and *Lutra lutra*.

第四节 野生动物保护等级标准
Section Ⅳ Grading Standard of Wildlife Protection

你知道吗？
Do you know?

野生动物保护等级标准主要是针对濒危物种。濒危物种是指那些由任何内、外因素造成的，使其生存繁衍受到威胁的物种。近一二百年来，随着人口的快速增长，世界上许多种鸟类、哺乳动物等已完全灭绝或陷于濒危状态，还有一些物种低于最低存活数量而需要抢救性保护。

The grading standard of wildlife protection is mainly designed for endangered species. Endangered species are species whose survival and reproduction are threatened for any internal and external factors. Over the past one or two centuries, with the rapid growth of population, many birds and mammals in the world have been completely extinct or are endangered, and the number of some species is lower than the minimum survival number, thus needing rescue protection.

一、IUCN 濒危物种红皮书
I. IUCN Red List of Threatened Species

目前，国际上有多个濒危物种等级的划分标准，其中最重要的一个为世界自然保护联盟（IUCN）划分的标准。世界自然保护联盟成立于 1948 年 10 月，是目前世界上最大的自然保护团体。IUCN 的使命旨在影响、鼓励及协助全球各地的社会，保护自然的完整性与多样性，并确保在使用自然资源上的公平性，以及生态上的可持续发展。

世界自然保护联盟（IUCN）标识
logo of International Union for Conservation of Nature (IUCN)

Currently, there are many grading standards of endangered species in the world, and the most important one is the standard from the International Union for Conservation of Nature (IUCN). Founded in October 1948, IUCN is currently the largest conservation organization in the world. IUCN's mission is designed to influence, encourage and assist communities around the world in protecting the integrity and diversity of nature and ensuring fairness of the use of natural resources and ecologically sustainable development.

IUCN 自 20 世纪 60 年代开始发布濒危动物红皮书。最初 IUCN 红皮书仅包括陆生脊椎动物，后来红皮书开始收录无脊椎动物和植物，内容逐年增加，逐步发展为 IUCN 濒危物种红色名录。

IUCN began to publish the "Red List of Threatened Species" from the 1960s. The initial IUCN "Red List of Threatened Species" included only terrestrial vertebrates, and the later one began to embraced invertebrates and plants. The content increases year by year and gradually develops into what it is now.

根据物种受威胁的程度和估计灭绝风险，IUCN 划分的濒危物种等级分为 8 个类别：绝灭（EX）、野外绝灭（EW）、极危（CR）、濒危（EN）、易危（VU）、近危（NT）、无危（LC）、数据缺乏（DD）。

According to the degree of threatened species and the estimated risk of extinction, the endangered species are divided into 8 categories by IUCN: extinct (EX), extinct in the wild (EW), critically endangered (CR), endangered (EN), vulnerable (VU), near threatened (NT), least concern (LC), and data deficient (DD).

二、CITES 附录标准
Ⅱ. CITES Appendix Standards

为了控制野生动植物国际贸易，多个国家于 1973 年在美国首都华盛顿签署了《濒危野生动植物种国际贸易公约》（CITES）。截至 2011 年 7 月，有 175 个国家签署了该公约。我国是这个公约的缔约国之一。CITES 将其管制的国际贸易野生动植物物种分别列入 CITES 的附录 1、附录 2 和附录 3 中，其中对被列入附录 1 的物种的国际贸易管控最为严格。CITES 附录标准相对于 IUCN 标准宽松。

In order to control international trade in wild animals and plants, many countries signed the *Convention on International Trade in Endangered Species of Wild Fauna and Flora* (CITES) in the US capital Washington in 1973. By July 2011, 175 countries have signed CITES. China is one of contracting parties of this convention. CITES includes the wild animal and plant species involved in the international trade under its jurisdiction in its Appendix 1, Appendix 2 and Appendix 3. The international trade involving species included in Appendix 1 is controlled most strictly. The CITES appendix standards are relatively more relaxed than the IUCN standard.

三、我国物种保护等级标准
Ⅲ. Grading Standard of Species Protection in China

1. 国家重点保护野生动物
1. National Key Protected Wildlife

《中华人民共和国野生动物保护法》（简称《野生动物保护法》）规定，国家对珍贵、濒危的野生动物实行重点保护。国家重点保护的野生动物名录及其调整，由国务院野生动物行政主管部门制定，报国务院批准公布。在 1988 年颁布的《国家重点保护野生动物名录》中使用了两个保护等级。我国特产稀有或濒临灭绝的野生动物被列为一级保护，而数量较少或有一定灭绝危险的野生动物被列为二级保护。

According to *Law of the People's Republic of China on the Protection of Wildlife* (hereinafter referred to as *Wildlife Protection Law*), the State shall give special protection to the species of wildlife which are rare or near extinction. Lists or revised lists of wildlife under national special protection shall be drawn up by the department of wildlife administration under the State Council and announced after being submitted to and approved by the State Council. Two protection levels were adopted in the *List of National Key Protected Wildlife* issued in 1988. The endemic rare or endangered wildlife in China is listed as national first-grade protected animals, while wild animals that survive in small numbers or that face the risk of extinction are listed as second-grade protected animals.

2. 地方重点保护野生动物
2. Local Key Protected Wildlife

地方重点保护野生动物，是指国家重点保护野生动物以外，由省、自治区、直辖市重点保护的野生动物。地方重点保护的野生动物名录，由省、自治区、直辖市政府制定并公布，报国务院备案。

The wildlife under special local protection, being different from the wildlife under special state protection, refers to the wildlife specially protected by provinces, autonomous regions or municipalities directly under the Central Government. Lists of wildlife under special local protection shall be drawn up and announced by the governments of provinces, autonomous regions or municipalities directly under the Central Government and shall be submitted to the State Council for the record.

在各省、自治区、直辖市公布的《地方重点保护野生动物名录》中，地方重点保护野生动物的保护等级一般也分为一级和二级两个等级。

In the *Lists of Local Key Protected Wildlife* issued at the provincial, autonomous regional and municipal level, local key protected wildlife is usually classified into first and second level.

四、我国对"三有动物"的保护
IV. Protection of Animals Which Are Beneficial or of Important Economic or Scientific Value

为了加强对我国国家和地方重点保护野生动物以外的陆生野生动物资源的保护和管理，根据《野生动物保护法》第九条，即"国家保护的有益的或者有重要经济、科学研究价值的陆生野生动物名录及其调整，由国务院野生动物行政主管部门制定并公布"的规定，国家林业局于 2000 年 8 月 1 日发布实施《国家保护的有益的或者有重要经济、科学研究价值的陆生野生动物名录》（简称"三有名录"）。"三有名录"共包括兽纲 6 目 14 科 88 种，鸟纲 18 目 61 科 707 种，两栖纲 3 目 10 科 291 种，爬行纲 2 目 20 科 395 种，昆虫纲 17 目 72 科 120 属另 110 种，合计 5 纲 46 目 177 科 1481 种及昆虫 120 属的所有种和另外 110 种。

In order to strengthen the protection and management of terrestrial wildlife resources other than the wildlife under special national and local protection, according to Article IX of the *Wildlife Protection Law*, namely: "Lists or revised lists of terrestrial wildlife under state protection, which are beneficial or of important economic or scientific value, shall be drawn up and announced by the department of wildlife administration under the State Council," the State Forestry Administration released the *List of Terrestrial Wildlife Which Are Beneficial or of Important Economic or Scientific Value under State Protection* (referred to as the "List") on August 1, 2000. The List covers a total of 88 species, 14 families and 6 orders of beasts; 707 species, 61 families and 18 orders of birds; 291 species, 10 families and 3 orders of amphibians; 395 species, 20 families and 2 orders of reptiles; and additional 110 species and 120 genuses, 72 families and 17 orders of insecta. Totally, there are 1,481 species, 177 families, 46 orders, and 5 classes, plus all the species of the 120 genuses and the additional 110 species of insects.

研究性学习
Investigative Study

　　请通过查阅资料，说出 2 种以上的"三有动物"，并以"三有动物"为对象，讲一则有趣的童话故事。
Consult references to name over 2 "animals which are beneficial or of important economic or scientific value", and tell an interesting fairy tale with such animals.

第四章　我国野生动物保护卓有成效
Chapter Ⅳ　Effective Wildlife Protection in China

　　以物种濒危和灭绝为典型特征的生物多样性丧失是当前世界所面临的全球性危机之一，生物多样性丧失对我国的生态环境安全有重要影响。为此我国在野生动物的保护与管理方面做出了很多努力。近 10 年调查监测的数据显示，我国珍稀濒危陆生野生动物的种群已经基本扭转了持续下降的态势，一批极度濒危的陆生野生动物物种正逐步摆脱灭绝的风险。本章我们共同来了解一下我国野生动物保护的成效吧。

Loss of biodiversity, represented by the endangerment and extinction of threatened species, is one of the global crises facing the world now. It has a significant impact on the eco-environmental security of China. Therefore, China has made many efforts in the protection and management of wildlife. Nearly a decade of investigation and monitoring data shows that China has basically reversed the declining trend in rare and endangered terrestrial wildlife species and a number of critically endangered species of terrestrial wildlife are gradually getting rid of the risk of extinction. In this chapter, we will look at the effectiveness of wildlife protection in China.

第一节　野生动物保护形成五大管理体系
Section Ⅰ　Five Management Systems of Wildlife Protection

你知道吗?
Do you know?

　　近十几年来，我国野生动物保护管理工作不断加强，形成了野生动物保护的五大管理体系。

Over the past decade, China has constantly strengthened wildlife protection and management to finally form five management systems of wildlife protection.

一、以自然保护区为主体的野外保护体系
I. Nature Reserve-based Wildness Protection System

截至 2014 年年底，全国自然保护区总数为 2729 个，总面积 14699 万公顷，其中自然保护区陆地面积约占国土面积的 14.84%。其中，国家级自然保护区 428 个，面积约 9652 万公顷。我国还建立了近 5 万处自然保护小区。目前，85% 以上的国家重点保护野生动物种群得到有效保护。湿地公园、森林公园的建设也不断得到加强。至 2013 年 10 月，我国国际重要湿地总数达 46 处。

By the end of 2014, there had been a total of 2,729 nature reserves in China, covering a total area of 146.99 million hectares, whose land area accounted for about 14.8% of the national land area. Among them, there were 428 national nature reserves, with an area of about 96.52 million hectares. China has also set up nearly 50,000 smaller nature reserves. Currently, more than 85% of the wildlife populations under national special protection are effectively protected. The construction of wetland parks and forest parks also continue to be strengthened. By October 2013, the total number of wetlands of international importance in China had climbed to 46.

二、野生动物救护繁育体系
Ⅱ. Wildlife Rescue and Breeding System

1980 年以来，我国对已有的濒危物种以各种形式进行保护，建立了华南虎、金丝猴、大熊猫、朱鹮、丹顶鹤等数十个濒危野生动物救护与繁育中心，达到了非常好的保护效果。

Since 1980, China has been protecting the existing endangered species in various ways, establishing dozens of rescue and breeding centers for endangered species such as *Panthera tigris amoyensis*, *Rhinopithecus*, *Ailuropoda melanoleuca*, *Nipponia nippon*, and *Grus japonensis*. Good protection effects have been achieved.

位于黑龙江省牡丹江市海林市境内的中国横道河子猫科动物饲养繁育中心（包含哈尔滨东北虎林园）是目前世界上最大的东北虎人工饲养繁育基地。1986 年该中心建立时仅有 8 只东北虎种虎，至 2010 年，该中心东北虎已达 1000 余只。

Located in Hailin, Mudanjiang City, Heilongjiang Province, the Hengdaohezi Breeding Center of Feline Animals in China (including the Harbin *Panthera tigris altaica* Park) is the largest artificial breeding base of *Panthera tigris altaica* in the world. In 1986, there were only 8 breeding *Panthera tigris altaica* when the center was established. By 2010, there had been more than 1,000 *Panthera tigris altaica* at the center.

　　国家林业局甘肃濒危动物保护中心（原名甘肃濒危野生动物繁育中心）位于古丝绸之路重镇——甘肃省武威市凉州区东北部，总面积98平方千米，全境属腾格里沙漠西南缘。 中心先后引进和繁育赛加羚羊、普氏野马、金丝猴、野骆驼等濒危珍稀野生动物43种400多头（只、匹），其中国家一二级保护动物31种，300多头（只、匹）。特别是普氏野马表现出良好的适应性和繁殖能力，已发展到75匹，2010年成功组织实施了首次试验性放归，并在野外成功繁殖幼驹1匹；金丝猴迁地保护成功繁育，两次赴日本展出、合作研究；赛加羚羊人工驯养繁育取得重要进展，至2013年存养赛加羚羊170余只。野生双峰驼是世界级濒危物种，现有16峰野生双峰驼，是国内最大的人工饲养种群，2012年9月顺利完成了2峰野骆驼全国首次试验性放归。

The Endangered Animal Protection Center of Gansu under the State Forestry Administration (formerly the Breeding Center of Endangered Wildlife in Gansu) is located in the northeast part of Liangzhou District, Wuwei City, Gansu Province, which is an important city on the ancient Silk Road. It covers a total area of 98 km^2 and located entirety in the southwestern edge of the Tengger Desert. The center introduced and bred more than 400 heads of rare and endangered wild animals belonging to 43 species, including *Saiga tatarica*, *Equus ferus* ssp. *przewalskii*, *Rhinopithecus*, and *Camelus bactrianus*. Among them, there were 31 national protected species grade Ⅰ and Ⅱ, involving more than 300 heads of animals. Especially, *Equus ferus* ssp. *przewalskii* has showed good adaptability and reproductive capability and has increased to 75 heads. In 2010, the first experimental release of *Equus ferus* ssp. *przewalskii* into the wild was successfully organized and implemented, and one young foal was successfully bred in the wild; *Rhinopithecus* under ex-situ protection were successfully bred and were exhibited and used for collaborative research in Japan twice; important progress was made in the artificial domestication and breeding of *Saiga tatarica* and more than 170 *Saiga tatarica* was raised by 2013. *Camelus bactrianus* is a globally endangered species. Now the center has 16 *Camelus bactrianus*, which form the largest artificially bred population in the country. In September 2012, the first experimental release of 2 *Camelus bactrianus* was successfully completed in the country.

三、野生动物保护科技支撑体系
Ⅲ. Scientific and Technological Support System of Wildlife Protection

　　在各级政府的大力支持下，各相关科研机构、高等院校、野生动物保护机构积极开展野生动物保护研究和科技攻关，为野生动物保护管理提供有效的科技支持和服务。
Under the strong support of governments at all levels, relevant research institutions, universities, and wildlife protection agencies are active in conducting studies and tackling hard-nut problems in wildlife protection to provide effective technological support and services for the management of wildlife protection.

我国野生动物科研体系由三级构成，包括中央级研究机构，如国家林业局全国野生动植物研究与发展中心、国家林业局虎保护研究中心、中国科学院动物研究所、中国科学院昆明动物研究所、中国林业科学研究院资源昆虫研究所，教育部所属相关高等院校，如东北林业大学野生动物资源学院、北京林业大学自然保护区学院；省级研究机构，如省级林业科研院所和相关大专院校，如黑龙江省野生动物研究所、广东省昆虫研究所（又名华南濒危动物研究所）、陕西省动物研究所（又名西北濒危动物研究所）；基层研究机构，如自然保护区管理部门所设置的研究机构等。在大熊猫、朱鹮、雉类、虎、灵长类、鹿类、羚羊类、鹤类、扬子鳄等重要物种的生态生物学及繁育，野生动物疫源疫病监测防控等研究方面有较好的研究基础和优秀的研究团队。

China's wildlife research system consists of three levels, namely research institutions at the central level, such as the National Wildlife Research and Development Center of the State Forestry Administration, Tiger protection Research Center of the State Forestry Administration the Institute of Zoology with the Chinese Academy of Sciences, Kunming Institute of Zoology with the Chinese Academy of Sciences, and the Research Institute of Resources Insects of the Chinese Academy of Forestry, and institutions of higher learning affiliated to the Ministry of Education, like the College of Wildlife Resources of the Northeast Forestry University, and the College of Nature Conservation of Beijing Forestry University; provincial research institutions, such as provincial forestry research institutes and related institutions of higher learning, including the Wildlife Institute of Heilongjiang Province, Guangdong Entomological Institute (also known as the South China Institute of Endangered animals), and Shaanxi Institute of Zoology (also known as the Northwest Institute of Endangered Zoological Species); and grassroots research institutions, such as those set up by nature reserve administrations. These institutions provide good foundation and excellent teams for the research of eco-biology and breeding of important species like *Ailuropoda melanoleuca*, *Nipponia nippon*, *Phasianidae*, *Panthera tigris*, *Primates*, *Cervidae*, *Antelope*, *Gruidae*, and *Alligator sinensis* and the research on prevention and control of wildlife epidemics.

四、野生动物保护执法监管体系
IV. Enforcement and Regulation System of Wildlife Protection

我国国家林业局设有野生动植物保护与自然保护区管理司，专门负责全国陆生野生动物的保护管理工作；我国农业部渔业局专门负责全国水生野生动物的保护管理工作。各省级林业主管部门内均设有专门的陆生野生动物保护管理机构。

The State Forestry Administration has set up the Management Division of Wildlife Protection and Nature Reserves to be responsible for the protection and management of terrestrial wildlife in the country; the Bureau of Fisheries of the Ministry of Agriculture is responsible for the protection and management of aquatic wildlife in the country. The provincial forestry authorities all have a special protection and management agency of terrestrial wildlife.

1980 年我国加入《濒危野生动植物种国际贸易公约》以后，经过三十多年的努力，我国的濒危野生动植物国际贸易监管和履约工作取得全面进步，贸易监管体系基本建立，履约法律法规体系趋于完备，进出口管理全面加强，履约国际影响不断扩大，公众保护意识显著提高。我国各级森林公安机关对国内野生动物走私以及非法贸易等违法行为也进行了坚决打击。

Since China joined the *Convention on International Trade in Endangered Species of Wild Fauna and Flora* in 1980, comprehensive progress has been made in the regulation and convention performance on international trade in endangered wildlife over the past three decades of efforts. China has basically established its trade regulation system, completed the legal system of convention compliance, and fully strengthened its import and export management. As a result, the international influence of China's compliance with the convention continues to expand and the public awareness of wildlife protection has been significantly improved. The forest public security organs at all levels in the country also resolutely fight against smuggling, illegal trade and other illegal activities of the domestic terrestrial wildlife.

五、陆生野生动物疫源疫病监测防控体系
V. Monitoring, Prevention and Control System of Terrestrial Wildlife Epidemic Sources and Diseases

野生动物不仅是宝贵的自然资源，而且是天然的"病原库"，是狂犬病、鼠疫、高致病性禽流感等许多人兽共患病的携带者和自然宿主，严重威胁珍稀濒危野生动物的保护，甚至直接威胁家养动物、人类的生命健康。野生动物疫源疫病监测工作十分重要。2005 年国家林业局依托国家林业局森林病虫害防治总站成立了国家林业局野生动物疫源疫病监测总站，负责全国野生动物疫源疫病监测工作。

Wildlife is not only a valuable natural resource but also a natural "pathogen library". Wild animals are carriers and natural hosts of many zoonotic diseases, such as rabies, plague, and highly pathogenic avian influenza. These diseases can seriously threaten the protection of rare and endangered wildlife and even directly threaten the life and health of domesticated animals and humans. Monitoring wildlife epidemic sources and diseases is extremely important. In 2005, the State Forestry Administration built the General Monitoring Center of Wildlife Epidemic Sources and Diseases on the basis of the General Prevention and Control Center of Forest Pests and Diseases. The General Monitoring Center is responsible for the monitoring of national wildlife epidemic sources and diseases.

至 2013 年，我国已经建立了 350 处国家级、768 处省级和一大批地县级陆生野生动物疫源疫病的监测站。布设了监测点和巡查路线近万处。在禽流感等野生动物疫源疫病的防控中，陆生野生动物疫源疫病监测防控体系发挥了重要作用。

By 2013, China has already established 350 national, 768 provincial, and a large number of county-level monitoring centers of terrestrial wildlife epidemic sources and diseases. Nearly ten thousand monitoring points and patrol routes have been set up. In the prevention and control of wildlife epidemic sources and diseases such as avian flu, the monitoring, prevention and control system of terrestrial wildlife epidemic sources and diseases plays an important role.

拓展阅读
Extended Reading

监测的野生动物疫源疫病主要种类
Main Categories of Wildlife Epidemic Sources and Diseases to be Monitored

1. 鸟类
1. Birds

细菌性传染病：禽巴斯德氏菌病（禽霍乱）、肉毒梭菌中毒、沙门菌感染、结核病、丹毒等。
Bacterial infectious diseases: avian pasteurellosis (fowl cholera), Clostridium botulinum poisoning, salmonellosis, tuberculosis, erysipelas, etc.

病毒性传染病：禽流感、冠状病毒感染、副黏病毒感染、禽痘、鸭瘟、新城疫、东部马脑炎、西尼罗河病毒感染、网状内皮增生病毒感染等。
Viral infectious diseases: avian influenza, coronavirus infection, paramyxovirus infection, fowl pox, duck plague, Newcastle disease, Eastern equine encephalitis, West Nile virus infection, Reticuloendotheliosis viral infection, etc.

衣原体病：禽衣原体病（鸟疫）等。
Chlamydia: avian chlamydiosis (ornithosis), etc.

立克次氏体病：Q 热病等。

Rickettsial disease: Q fever, etc.

2. 兽类

2. Beasts

细菌性传染病：鼠疫、猪链球菌病、结核病、兔热、布鲁氏菌病、炭疽、巴斯德氏菌病等。

Bacterial infectious diseases: plague, swine streptococcus, tuberculosis, tularemia, brucellosis, anthrax, Pasteurella disease, etc.

病毒性传染病：流感、口蹄疫、副黏病毒感染、汉坦病毒感染、冠状病毒感染、狂犬病、犬瘟热、登革热、黄热病、马尔堡病毒感染、艾博拉病毒感染、西尼罗河病毒感染、猴 B 病毒感染等。

Viral infectious diseases: influenza, aftosa, paramyxovirus infection, hantavirus infection, coronavirus infection, rabies, distemper, dengue fever, yellow fever, Marburg virus infection, Ebola virus infection, West Nile virus infection, simian B virus infection, etc.

3. 其他可引起野生动物发病或死亡的不明原因的疫病

3. Other Diseases That Can Cause Unexplained Wildlife Morbidity or Mortality

4. 国家要求监测的疫源疫病

4. Epidemic Sources and Diseases That must Be Monitored under the State Requirement

野生动物疫源疫病监测的主要野生动物物种
Main Wildlife Species under Monitoring of Wildlife Epidemic Sources and Diseases

兽类（灵长类、有蹄类、啮齿类、食肉类和翼手类等）和鸟类，特别是候鸟等迁徙物种和珍贵濒危野生动物。

Beasts (primates, ungulates, rodents, carnivores, chiropters, etc.) and birds, especially migratory species and rare and endangered wildlife, including migratory birds.

野生动物疫源疫病监测的主要区域
Main Areas for Monitoring of Wildlife Epidemic Sources and Diseases

监测物种的集中分布区域，如：集中繁殖地、越冬地、夜栖地、取食地及迁徙中途停歇地等。

Centralized distribution areas of monitored species, such as: centralized breeding sites, wintering site, roosting sites, foraging sites, and migratory stopover sites, etc.

监测物种与人和饲养动物密切接触的重点区域。

Key areas where the monitored species have close contact with human beings and domesticated animals.

曾经发生过重大疫病的区域及周边地区。

Areas where serious epidemic diseases once occurred and their surroundings.

近些年来，我国野生动物疫源疫病监测部门按照"第一时间发现、第一现场处置"原则，有效控制了候鸟高致病性禽流感、旱獭鼠疫、野鸟禽霍乱、鼬獾犬瘟热等多起突发野生动物疫情，为维护公共卫生安全和社会稳定做出了重要贡献。

In recent years, the monitoring departments of wildlife epidemic sources and diseases in China have effectively controlled the sudden outbreaks of many animal plagues including highly pathogenic avian influenza of migratory birds, marmot plague, wild fowl cholera, and ferret badger distemper in accordance with the principles of "discovering in first time and disposing on site", making important contributions to the broad effort to maintain public health and safety and social stability.

第二节　我国野生动物保护代表性成果
Section Ⅱ Representative Achievements in Wildlife Protection in China

目前，我国230多种野生动物已建立了稳定的人工繁育种群。

At present, more than 230 species of wild animals in China have established stable artificial breeding populations.

一、重要物种保护卓有成效
I. Effective Protection of Important Species

至 2013 年，我国重要物种的保护卓有成效。朱鹮由 1981 年时发现的 7 只，发展到 2000 多只；扬子鳄从 20 世纪 80 年代野生种群仅剩 300 多条的情况下，发展到 10000 条以上；大熊猫野外种群数量已达到 1596 只、人工繁育种群数量为 341 只；东北虎的野外种群从 2000 年的 12~16 头增长到了 18~22 头；海南坡鹿种群数量由仅存的 26 只恢复到了 1780 只，同时其栖息地也扩大了。

By 2013, the protection of important species had been effective in China. The population of *Nippon nippon* rose from 7 when they were found in 1981 to over 2000; the population of *Alligator sinensis* rose from an estimated mere 300 in the 1980s to more than 10,000; the wild population of *Ailuropoda melanoleuca* had reached 1596, which included 341 artificially bred animals; the wild population of *Panthera tigris altaica* rose from 12–16 in 2000 to 18–22; the population of *Cervus eldii* rose from a mere 26 to 1,780 and had expanded habitats.

20 世纪 80 年代我国开始从国外引进在本土曾一度灭绝的动物如赛加羚羊、普氏野马、野骆驼、麋鹿等进行人工驯养。目前甘肃濒危动物保护中心半散放的赛加羚羊种群个体数量已经达到 170 头左右。这些珍稀动物种群数量的恢复对我国濒危动物保护工作有着非常积极的意义和研究价值。

Since the 1980s, China has begun to introduce from abroad animals that had gone extinct in China, such as *Saiga tatarica, Equus ferus* ssp. *przewalskii, Camelus bactrianus*, and *Elaphurus davidianus* for artificial domestication. Now, the semi-wild *Saiga tatarica* population at the Protection Center of Endangered Animals in Gansu has reached about 170. The restored populations of these rare and endangered animals are of positive significance and provide positive research value for the protection of endangered animals in China.

二、对重要野生动物成功放归
II. Successful Release of Important Wildlife to Nature

目前，我国已对朱鹮、麋鹿、扬子鳄、普氏野马、大熊猫等 14 种野生动物成功实施放归自然工作。在山东省蓬莱市人工繁殖了斑海豹，并在 2012 年 4 月底成功将其放归自然。

At present, China has begun the release of 14 wildlife species, including *Nipponia nippon, Elaphurus davidianus, Alligator sinensis, Equus ferus* ssp. *przewalskii*, and *Ailuropoda melanoleuca*, to nature. *Phoca largha* that were artificially bred in Penglai, Shandong Province, were successfully released to nature in the end of April, 2012.

1. 麋鹿放归自然

1. Release of *Elaphurus davidianus* to Nature

1986 年 8 月 14 日，由世界自然基金会（WWF）、我国原林业部与英国政府签订了麋鹿引返中国的协议，从英国 7 家皇家动物园中挑选了 39 头麋鹿，空运至江苏大丰，并在大丰市境内建立了麋鹿自然保护区。麋鹿终于结束了百年之久的侨居生涯，回归到了它们的原生地。 截至 1998 年春，大丰麋鹿种群数量已达到 354 头。1998 年 11 月 5 日，8 头麋鹿被放归自然。大丰麋鹿自然保护区又分别于 2002 年、2003 年和 2006 年实施了野生放归自然试验，算上 1998 年的放归活动，4 次共放归麋鹿 53 头。截至 2008 年产仔期结束，野外麋鹿种群数量已达到 118 头。这一保护成果同时表明我国野生麋鹿种群恢复工程已获成功，链接了 100 多年以来世界上没有野生麋鹿种群的生命环缺，并可改善保护区内的生物多样性，优化森林生态系统，促进人与自然和谐发展。

On August 14, 1986, the World Wildlife Fund (WWF), the former Ministry of Forestry of China, and the British government signed an agreement on the reintroduction of *Elaphurus davidianus* back to China. A total of 39 deer were selected from 7 royal zoos in Britain and were transported by air to Dafeng, Jiangsu Province, where a nature reserve was built for *Elaphurus davidianus*. *Elaphurus davidianus* finally concluded its expatriate experience for a century and returned to their native place. By the spring of 1998, the population of *Elaphurus davidianus* in Dafeng reached 354. On November 5, 1998, 8 *Elaphurus davidianus* were released to the nature. Dafeng Nature Reserve of *Elaphurus davidianus* conducted the release experiments in 2002, 2003, and 2006, respectively. Altogether 53 deer were released in the four experiments, including release in 1998. By the end of the birth period in 2008, the wild population of *Elaphurus davidianus* reached 118. This result has also showed that population of wild *Elaphurus davidianus* has been successfully restored in China, and the history of absence of the life gap of the wild *Elaphurus davidianus* population in nature over 100 years has been ended. The forest ecosystem has been optimized, and the harmonious development of human and nature has been promoted.

2. 普氏野马放归自然

2. Release of *Equus ferus* ssp. *przewalskii* to Nature

普氏野马是现今唯一存活的野生马，是我国的原产物种，在我国已灭绝数十年。为拯救该物种，并在其原分布区重建野生种群，国家林业局于 20 世纪 80 年代后期开始"野马还乡计划"，从国外引进野马种群在新疆和甘肃进行人工繁育，取得成功，目前我国普氏野马总数已达 300 匹。

Equus ferus ssp. *przewalskii* is now the only surviving wild horse species and is also a native species in China. It had been extinct in China for decades. To save the species and to rebuild its wild population in its original distribution area, the State Forestry Administration launched the "Return Program of *Equus ferus* ssp. *przewalskii* " program in the late 1980s. The program was intended to introduce the population of *Equus ferus* ssp. *przewalskii* from abroad for artificial breeding in Xinjiang and Gansu. With success of the program, now the number of *Equus ferus* ssp. *przewalskii* in China has reached about 300.

2012 年 9 月 6 日上午，普氏野马第二次放归自然活动暨野骆驼首次试验性放归自然活动在甘肃省敦煌市西湖国家自然保护区举行，共有 21 匹普氏野马和四峰野骆驼重返大自然。而两年前这里放归的 7 匹马儿已经完全适应了自然的生活，并且产下了一匹小马驹。我国还在新疆的卡拉麦里自然保护区放归了普氏野马，也取得了成功。

In the morning of September 6, 2012, the second release of *Equus ferus* ssp. *przewalskii* to nature and the first experimental release of *Camelus ferus* were conducted in Gansu Dunhuang West Lake National Nature Reserve. A total of 21 *Equus ferus* ssp. *przewalskii* and 4 *Camelus ferus* were released back to nature. Of those release two years ago, 7 horses have completely adapted themselves to the natural life and gave birth to a foal. *Equus ferus* ssp. *przewalskii* were also released in the Karamaili Nature Reserve in Xinjiang and that was also a successful release.

3. 大熊猫放归自然
3. Release of the *Ailuropoda melanoleuca* to Nature

2012 年 10 月 11 日，国家林业局和四川省政府在四川省雅安市石棉县举行大熊猫放归自然活动，将我国第一只经过系统野化培训的人工繁育雄性大熊猫 "淘淘" 放归到栗子坪自然保护区内。此举标志着我国大熊猫保护工作进入了新的发展阶段，是我国野生动物保护的又一个重要里程碑。2013 年 11 月 6 日，国家林业局和四川省林业厅在四川省雅安市石棉县栗子坪自然保护区联合举办了 "小相岭大熊猫放归基地" 揭牌和大熊猫 "张想" 放归活动，将经过系统野化培训的雌性大熊猫 "张想" 放入基地的适应圈中，待其适应放归环境后，自然进入野生环境，回归自然家园。大熊猫 "淘淘" 和 "张想" 相继放归自然，标志着我国大熊猫保护已经从 "扩繁保种" 发展到 "野外小

（陈建伟摄）
中国野生动物保护的功绩——大熊猫
野外放归
an achievement in China wildlife protection —
release of *Ailuropoda melanoleuca* to the wild
(Credit: Chen Jianwei)

种群复壮"的新阶段，开辟了大熊猫保护事业的新纪元。

On October 11, 2012, the State Forestry Administration and the Sichuan Provincial Government held an event to mark the release of an *Ailuropoda melanoleuca* into the wild in Shimian County, Ya'an City, Sichuan Province. The first artificially bred male *Ailuropoda melanoleuca* named "Taotao" that had received systematic wild training was released to Liziping Nature Reserve. The event indicated that the protection of *Ailuropoda melanoleuca* in China had entered into a new stage of development, and the event was another important milestone in the protection of wild animals in China. On November 6, 2013, the State Forestry Administration and the Forestry Department of Sichuan jointly held the inauguration ceremony of "Release Base of *Ailuropoda melanoleuca* in Xiaoxiangling Mountain"and the release event of *Ailuropoda melanoleuca* named "Zhang Xiang" During the event, the female *Ailuropoda melanoleuca* "Zhang Xiang", which had received systematic wild training, was released into the adaptation circle in the base and would later go further into the wild environment after it adapted to the nature. The release of "Taotao" and "Zhang Xiang" to nature marked that the protection of *Ailuropoda melanoleuca* in China had developed from "propagation for conservation" to the new stage of "rejuvenation of wild small population", and a new era of *Ailuropoda melanoleuca* protection was opened.

研究性学习
Investigative Study

叙述野生动物放归自然的益处和困难。

Describe the benefits and difficulties of releasing wildlife to nature.

拓展阅读
Extended Reading

我国的湿地公园
Wetland Parks in China

在我国，湿地公园的定义，是指"以具有显著或特殊生态、文化、美学和生物多样性价值的湿地景观为主体，具有一定规模和范围，以保护湿地生态系统完整性、维护湿地生态过程和生态服务功能，并在此基础上以充分发挥湿地的多种功能效益、开展湿地合理利用为宗旨，可供公众浏览、休闲或进行科学、文化和教育活动的特定湿地区域"。湿地公园分国家湿地公园和省级湿地公园两个等级，其中国家湿地公园由国家林业局批准设立。湿地公园除了保护湿地生态系统完整性、维护湿地生态过程和生态服务功能外，兼有物种及其栖息地保护、生态旅游和生态环境教育功能。

In China, a wetland park is defined as "any special wetland area with a certain scale and scope of wetland landscape that has significant or special ecological, cultural, aesthetic and biological diversity value, for the purposes of protecting the wetland ecosystem integrity, maintaining wetland ecological processes and ecosystem services, and on this basis, giving full play to a variety of functional benefits of wetlands and rationally using wetlands, as well as serving as a site for public viewing, recreation or holding scientific, cultural and educational activities". Wetland park is divided into the two levels of national wetland park and provincial wetland park. The former is built under the approval of the State Forestry Administration. In addition to protecting the wetland ecosystem integrity and maintaining wetland ecological processes and ecosystem services, wetland parks can also be used for protection of species and their habitats, eco-tourism and eco-environmental education.

自 2005 年第一个国家湿地公园诞生以来，至 2012 年 12 月，国家林业局已经批准建立北京野鸭湖国家湿地公园、浙江杭州西溪国家湿地公园等 319 个国家湿地公园。

Since the birth of the first national wetland park in 2005, the State Forestry Administration had approved the establishment of 319 national wetland parks including Beijing Yeyahu National Wetland Park and Hangzhou Xixi National Wetland Park in Zhejiang by December 2012.

第三节 我国野生动物保护前景展望
Section Ⅲ Prospect of Wildlife Protection in China

我国各级政府对野生动物保护工作不断重视。在每年的"爱鸟周""野生动物保护宣传月"的活动中都有政府各级代表的身影，各界群众也踊跃参加野生动物保护活动。

Governments at all levels pay constant attention on wildlife protection. Government representatives at all levels are seen in activities like "Bird Week" and "Wildlife Protection Awareness Month". All walks of life also actively take part in wildlife protection activities.

一、各级政府、社会各界对野生动物保护工作不断重视
I. Governments at All Levels and People from All Walks of Life Attach Importance to Wildlife Protection

遍布全国的野生动物保护协会不断发展。中国野生动物保护协会 (CWCA) 于 1983 年 12 月在北京成立，是一个具有广泛代表性的野生动物保护组织，是中国科协所属全国性社会团体，常设办事机构为秘书处，行政上受国家林业局领导。它是由野生动物保护管理、科研教育、驯养繁殖、自然保护区工作者和广大野生动物爱好者组成的群众团体，其宗旨是推动中国野生动物保护事业的发展，为保护、拯救濒危、珍稀动物做出贡献。

Wildlife protection associations across the country continue to develop. Established in December 1983 in Beijing, China Wildlife Conservation Association (CWCA) is a broadly representative wildlife conservation organization and national social group affiliated to China Association for Science and Technology. It has a permanent office of secretariat and subject to the leadership of the State Administrative Forestry. It is an organization formed of people engaged in wildlife protection and management, research and education, domestication and breeding, and nature reserves, as well as the general wildlife enthusiasts, for the purpose of promoting the development of wildlife protection in China and making contributions to the protection and rescue of endangered and rare animals.

二、野生动物保护工作前途光明
Ⅱ. Promising Prospect of Wildlife Protection

我国目前正在加强生态文明建设，中央提出了建设美丽中国、秀美山川的目标。野生动物保护工作是生态文明建设中的重要一环，随着国家对生态文明建设的不断重视，相信我国的野生动物保护工作在未来会取得更大成就。我国野生动物保护工作前途光明。

China is currently strengthening the construction of ecological civilization. The Central Government has proposed the goal to construct a beautiful China and beautiful homeland. Wildlife protection is an important part of ecological civilization construction. As the state continues to attach importance to the construction of ecological civilization, it is sure that greater achievements will be made in the future undertaking of wildlife protection. The wildlife protection in China will be promising.

研究性学习
Investigative Study

　　同学们，你是否愿意参加中国野生动物保护协会，一旦加入该协会，你将采取哪些行动？

Would you like to join CWCA? What actions will you take when you join it?

拓展阅读
Extended Reading

了解几个著名野生动物保护组织
Understand Several Famous Wildlife Protection Organizations

1. 中国野生动物保护协会

1. CWCA

　　中国野生动物保护协会成立于 1983 年，是一个具有广泛代表性的野生动物保护组织。截至 2010 年年底，全国已有省、地、市、县级协会 773 个，拥有会员 34.5 万多人。它是由野生动物保护管理、科研教育、驯养繁殖、自然保护区工作者和广大野生动物爱好者组成的群众团体，其宗旨是推动中国野生动物保护事业的发展，为保护、拯救濒危、珍稀动物做出贡献。其主要任务是，组织会员贯彻国家保护野生动物的方针、法令，开展拯救和保护珍稀野生动物的宣传教育，开展保护野生动物的科学研究、学术交流，提供经营管理野生动物资源的技术业务咨询，筹募保护野生动物的资金，同各国自然保护组织和机构建立联系，参与有关国际合作与交流。

China Wildlife Conservation Association (CWCA)was founded in 1983. It is a broadly representative wildlife conservation organization. By the end of 2010, there had been 773 provincial and county-level wildlife protection associations in the country. With more than 345,000 members, CWCA is formed of people engaged in wildlife protection and management, research and education, domestication and breeding, and nature reserves, as well as the general wildlife enthusiasts, for the purpose of promoting the development of wildlife protection in China and making contributions to the protection and rescue of endangered and rare animals. Its main tasks are to organize the members to implement the national policy and decrees concerning wildlife protection, to carry out public education on the rescue and protection of rare wildlife, to carry out scientific research and academic exchanges on wildlife protection, to provide technical and business consulting on operation and management of wildlife resources, to raise funds to protect wildlife, to establish contact with nature conservation organizations and institutions around the world, and to participate in the relevant international cooperation and exchanges.

2. 世界自然基金会
2. WWF

世界自然基金会是在全球享有盛誉的、最大的独立性非政府环境保护组织之一。WWF1961 年成立，总部位于瑞士格朗。WWF 致力于保护世界生物多样性及生物的生存环境，它的使命是遏止地球自然环境的恶化，创造人类与自然和谐相处的美好未来。The World Wildlife Fund (WWF) is one of the largest independent non-governmental environmental organizations known worldwide. Founded in 1961 and headquartered in Gland, Switzerland, the WWF is committed to protecting biodiversity and biological habitats around the world. Its mission is to stop the degradation of natural environments on the planet and build harmony between mankind and nature for a better future.

3. 世界自然保护联盟
3. IUCN

著名的世界自然保护联盟是一个国际组织，专注于世界自然环境保护，致力于寻找当前迫切的环境与发展问题的实用解决方式。是政府及非政府机构都能参与合作的少数几个国际组织之一，于 1948 年 10 月在瑞士格朗成立。The International Union for Conservation of Nature (IUCN), a world-famous international organization, is dedicated to the protection of natural environment in the world and the search of practical solutions to solve the currently pressing environmental and development issues. It is one of the few international organizations that embrace both governmental and non-governmental members. It was established in October 1948 in Gland, Switzerland.

4. 国际野生生物保护学会
4. WCS

国际野生生物保护学会是一个保护野生生物为宗旨的公益组织。它通过教育，改变人们对自然的态度，让人们意识到动物和人类一样拥有同样的生存权利。The Wildlife Conservation Society (WCS) is a public interest organization to protect wildlife. It seeks to change people's attitude towards nature and help people realize that animals share the same right to life as humans through educational.

第五章　保护野生动物——中学生在行动
Chapter V Protecting Wildlife — Middle School Students in Action

保护野生动物迫在眉睫，任重道远，全社会都应该关注并行动起来，作为中学生的我们能做什么呢？本章开始，让我们共同探讨中学生们该做什么吧。

Protecting wildlife is an imminent and daunting task. The whole society should pay attention and take action. As middle school students, what can we do? Let's explore what contributions middle school students can make in this chapter.

第一节　身边的行动
Section I Actions around Us

一、野生动物保护宣传月
I. Wildlife Conservation Awareness Month

每年全国各地省级林业主管部门都组织开展野生动物保护宣传月活动。各地选定的野生动物保护宣传月时间不尽相同。在这个时间段内，中学生可以参与进来，采取各种宣传形式，传授野生动物知识，大力倡导保护野生动物。

野生动物保护宣传知识
public knowledge of wildlife protection

Every year, provincial forestry authorities across the country organize the activity of Wildlife Conservation Awareness Month. The time it takes place varies with the place, but in whatever period is chosen, middle school students can get involved in various forms of publicity to impart knowledge about wildlife and advocate wildlife protection.

二、爱鸟周
Ⅱ. Bird Week

"爱鸟周"源于 1981 年，最初是为保护迁徙于中日两国间的候鸟而设立。1992 年国务院批准的《陆生野生动物保护条例》，将爱鸟周以法规的形式确定下来。确定在每年的 4 月至 5 月初的某一个星期为爱鸟周，在此期间开展各种宣传教育活动。由于我国幅员辽阔，南北气候不同，各地选定的爱鸟周时间也不尽相同。

Dating back to 1981, the Bird Week was initially designed for the protection of migratory birds between China and Japan. The State Council approved the *Regulations on the Protection of Terrestrial Wildlife* in 1992, establishing the Bird Week by law. The regulations stipulates that a week between April to early May should be chosen as the Bird Week each year, during which a variety of promotional and educational activities will be carried out. Due to the vast territory of China and the different climates in the north and the south, the Bird Week comes at different time in different places.

爱鸟周宣传手绘画
publicity paintings for the Bird Week

爱鸟周我们的承诺
our commitments during the Bird Week

三、世界野生动植物日
Ⅲ. World Wildlife Day

2013 年 12 月 20 日，第 68 届联合国大会将每年 3 月 3 日确定为"世界野生动植物日"，2014 年 3 月 3 日为首个"世界野生动植物日"。

On December 20, 2013, the sixty-eighth session of the United Nations General Assembly chose March 3 as the "World Wildlife Day". March 3, 2014 was the first "World Wildlife Day".

四、全球老虎日
Ⅳ. International Tiger Day

2010 年 1 月，在泰国召开的老虎保护亚洲部长级会议提出，将每年的 7 月 29 日设为"全球老虎日"。2010 年 11 月，在俄罗斯圣彼得堡召开的"保护老虎国际论坛"（即老虎峰会）上，来自孟加拉人民共和国、不丹王国、柬埔寨王国、中华人民共和国、印度共和国、印度尼西亚共和国、老挝人民民主共和国、马来西亚、缅甸联邦共和国、尼泊尔联邦民主共和国、俄罗斯联邦、泰王国和越南社会主义共和国 13 个全球野生虎分布国的政府首脑和代表会聚一堂，通过了一项重大的联合行动计划——"全球野生虎种群恢复计划"，并联合发表了《全球野生虎分布国首脑宣言》，倡议共同努力促进野生虎及栖息地的保护，并将每年的 7 月 29 日定为"全球老虎日"。

An Asian ministerial conference on tiger conservation held in Thailand in January 2010 proposed to choose July 29 as the "International Tiger Day". In November 2010, at the "International Forum on Tiger Conservation" (i.e. Tiger Summit) in St. Petersburg, Russia, government leaders and representatives from 13 countries where wild tigers are distributed, including the People's Republic of Bangladesh, the Kingdom of Bhutan, the Kingdom Cambodia, the People's Republic of China, the Republic of India, the Republic of Indonesia, the Lao People's Democratic Republic, Malaysia, the Republic of the Union of Myanmar, the Federal Democratic of Republic Nepal, the Russian Federation, the Kingdom of Thailand, and the Socialist Republic of Vietnam, came together and passed a major joint action plan titled the "Global Tiger Recovery Program". They also jointly issued *The St. Petersburg Declaration on Tiger Conservation*, proposing to promote the protection of wild tigers and their habitats through joint efforts, and chose July 29 as the "International Tiger Day".

研究性学习
Investigative Study

请谈一谈你参加过哪些保护野生动物的活动，介绍一下具体的过程及效果。
Please talk about any wildlife protection activities that you joined and describe the processes and effects.

拓展阅读
Extended Reading

我国各地爱鸟周
Bird Weeks around China

　　我国部分省（市、自治区）爱鸟周时间如下：内蒙古自治区为5月1—7日；辽宁省为4月22—28日；吉林省为4月22—28日；黑龙江省为4月的第四周；北京市为4月1—7日；天津市为4月的第三周；山西省为4月1—7日；河北省为5月1—7日；山东省为4月23—29日；河南省为4月21—27日；新疆维吾尔自治区为5月6日的所在周；甘肃省为4月24—30日；宁夏回族自治区为4月1—7日；陕西省为4月11—17日；青海省为5月1—7日；上海市为4月4—10日；江苏省为4月20—26日；安徽省为5月1—7日；江西省为4月1—7日；浙江省为4月4—10日；湖北省为4月1—7日；湖南省为4月1—7日；广东省为3月20—26日；海南省为3月20—26日；福建省为4月11—17日；广西壮族自治区为2月22—28日；贵州省为3月的第一周；四川省为4月2—8日；云南省为4月1—7日。

The Bird Weeks in some Chinese provinces (municipalities and autonomous regions) are as follows: May 1–7 for Inner Mongolia Autonomous Region; April 22–28 for Liaoning Province; April 22–28 for Jilin Province; the fourth week of April for Heilongjiang Province; April 1–7 for Beijing; the third week of April for Tianjin; April 1–7 for Shanxi Province; May 1–7 for Hebei Province; April 23 –29 for Shandong Province; April 21–27 for Henan Province; the week that contains May 6 for Xinjiang Uygur Autonomous Region; April 24–30 for Gansu Province; April 1–7 for Ningxia Hui Autonomous Region; April 11–17 for Shaanxi Province; May 1–7 for Qinghai Province; April 4–10 for Shanghai; April 20–26 for Jiangsu Province; May 1–7 for Anhui Province; April 1–7 for Jiangxi Province; April 4–10 for Zhejiang Province; April 1–7 for Hubei Province; April 1–7 for Hunan Province; March 20–26 for Guangdong Province; March 20–26 for Hainan Province; April 11–17 for Fujian Province; February 22–28 for Guangxi Zhuang Autonomous Region; the first week of March for Guizhou Province; April 2–8 for Sichuan Province; April 1–7 for Yunnan Province.

第二节　个人在野生动物保护中的责任和义务

Section II　The Individual's Responsibilities and Obligations in Wildlife Protection

一、学习野生动物保护知识

I. Acquiring Knowledge about Wildlife Protection

作为一名中学生，有必要学习一些野生动物保护的知识，以备不时之需。我们可以学习野生动物有哪些、野生动物保护的措施等知识，进而宣传与提高个人责任意识。一般来讲，野生动物保护措施有以下几种。

It is necessary for middle school student to acquire some knowledge about wildlife protection to be prepared for contingencies. We can learn about the species of wildlife and protection measures of wildlife and then publicize and raise awareness of individual responsibility. In general, the following wildlife protection measures are taken.

一要加强监督检查。督促各地迅速开展野生动物保护执法行动，形成强大声势，打击乱捕滥猎滥食野生动物和走私、非法经营野生动物产品的违法犯罪活动。

First, strengthen supervision and inspection. Urge on enforcement actions to protect wildlife rapidly and create a powerful momentum to against illegal and criminal activities such as reckless capturing and indiscriminate eating wildlife, smuggling and illegal operation of wildlife products.

二要切实强化野生动物分布区的野外巡护和看守。要在野生动物分布的山地、田林、湿地，组织力量加强巡护和看守，严厉打击乱捕滥猎野生动物行为，依法制止和惩处非法猎捕野生动物、损毁野生动物栖息地、干扰野生动物生息繁衍活动的行为，并收缴或清除兽夹、兽套等非法猎捕工具。

Second, earnestly strengthen field patrolling and guarding in wildlife distribution areas. Organize forces to strengthen patrolling and guarding in mountains land, field woodland, and wet land where wildlife distribute, crack down on reckless capturing and hunting for wildlife, deter and punish illegal hunting wildlife, and the behaviors that damage wildlife habitats and disturb survival and reproduction of wildlife by law, and confiscate or eliminate illegal hunting tools such as beast traps and snares.

三要全面检查野生动物经营利用场所，清理整顿非法经营利用行为。尤其是对餐馆饭店、花鸟市场、药用野生动物原材料集散地和其他野生动物及其产品经营较集中的场所，进行一次全面检查，对经营利用非法猎捕或走私的野生动物及其产品的，进行清理整顿，并依法惩处。

Third, fully inspect the operation and utilization sites of wildlife, and screen and rectify illegal business behaviors. Restaurants, hotels, bird and flower markets, distribution centers of wildlife as pharmaceutical raw materials, and places where concentrated wildlife and wildlife associated products business is carried out should be fully inspected. Screen and rectify illegal hunting and smuggling of wildlife and wildlife associated products, and punish the illegal operation and business according to law.

四要加强林业部门与海关、边防、运输等部门的协调行动，综合整治，严查走私、非法运输野生动物及其产品的行为。

Fourth, strengthen the coordinated actions of the Forestry Department with the Customs, Border Defense, and Transportation Departmet, perform comprehensive regulation, thoroughly investigate smuggling and illegal transport of wildlife.

五要加强野生动物保护宣传教育，更广泛地争取全社会的理解和支持，倡导保护新理念，提高广大人民群众的保护意识。发动人民群众关注、支持保护执法行动，形成群防群治的良好局面。

Fifth, strengthen the publicity and education of wildlife protection, win broad understanding and support of the whole society, advocate for new protection ideas, and improve the protection awareness of the masses. Mobilize people to pay attention to and support the law enforcement of wildlife protection, and create a favorable atmosphere of mass prevention and mass treatment.

二、积极参与野生动物保护
II. Actively Participate in Wildlife Protection

不滥食野生动物、积极参与救助受伤的野生动物、积极参与野生动物保护宣传、争取家人对野生动物保护工作的支持、做野生动物保护的小志愿者。主要包括以下四个方面：一是自觉抵制和动员父母、朋友抵制非法行为，不购买没有标识的野生动物产品，不滥食野生动物；二是及时举报乱捕滥猎滥食和非法出售野生动物产品的行为；三是参加生态旅游，参观游览野生动物园、自然博物馆，了解野生动物和自然保护知识，爱惜野生动物和自然环境；四是参加力所能及的野生动物保护宣传活动。

Do not eat wildlife recklessly; actively participate in rescuing injured wildlife, actively participate in wildlife protection advocacy, winning support from family for wildlife protection, and be a small volunteer for wildlife protection. Pay attention to the following four aspects: First, consciously resist illegal acts and mobilize your parents and friends to fight against them, do not buy any wildlife products not duly labeled, and do not eat wildlife recklessly; second, immediately report reckless capturing and eating of wildlife and illegal sale of wildlife products when you find these acts; third, participate in eco-tourism, visit safaris and nature museums, understand knowledge about wildlife and nature conservation, and love wildlife and the natural environment; fourth, participate in whatever wildlife conservation campaigns you can take part in within your power.

国家林业局野生动植物保护与自然保护区管理司原巡视员陈建伟教授
参加指导北京第二外国语学院附属中学学生的野生动物保护活动
Professor Chen Jianwei, Former Inspector in Management Division of Wildlife Protection and Nature Reserve under the State Forestry Administration, attending the wildlife protection activity of the High School Affiliated to Beijing International Studies University

研究性学习
Investigative Study

如果你遇到了一起正在猎杀国家一级保护动物东北虎的事件，你该如何处理？
If you find someone killing the national protected animal *Panthera tigris altaica*, what would you do?

拓展阅读
Extended Reading

高校野生动物保护专业
The Wildlife Protection Major in Higher Education

一、专业概况
Ⅰ. Major Profile

野生动物保护（代码：510205）属于农林牧渔大类，林业技术类。
Wildlife Protection (code: 510205) part of forestry technology under the umbrella of agriculture, forestry, animal husbandry and fishery.

野生动物保护专业主要学习森林资源经营管理、森林生态学、森林环境学、生物技术、动物学、野生动物组织解剖学、生物化学、动物遗传育种等基本知识，并受到相关实践方面的专业训练。
The Wildlife Protection major is mainly concerned with the basics of forest resource management, forest ecology, forest environmental science, biotechnology, zoology, wildlife tissue anatomy, biochemistry, animal genetics and breeding, etc., as well as relevant professional practice training.

二、培养目标
Ⅱ. Educational Goals

该专业主要培养具有野生动物保护与利用、自然保护区管理等方面的基本理论和专业知识，学成后能在与野生动物和自然保护区相关的行业从事生产管理等工作的高级技术应用性专门人才。
The major trains qualified talents in high-tech application who master basic theories and professional knowledge of wildlife protection and utilization and management of nature reserves and who can engage in the production and management of industries associated with wildlife and nature reserves after graduation.

三、知识技能
Ⅲ. Knowledge & Skills

通过学习，将具备以下几方面的能力。
After learning, the students are expected to master the following knowledge and skills.

1. 掌握生物学、畜牧学学科的基本理论、基本知识；
1. Basic theories and basic knowledge on biology and animal science;

2. 掌握野生动物无线电遥测技术、野生动物种群数量及自然保护区资源调查；
2. Wildlife radio telemetry technology, wildlife populations and survey of resources in nature reserves;

3. 具有野生动物繁育、保护、利用、疾病防治、检疫，动植物资源调查、监测及经营管理的初步能力；
3. Knowledge about breeding, protection, utilization, disease prevention, and quarantine of wildlife, and initial ability in survey, monitoring and management of animal and plant resources;

4. 熟悉我国野生动物保护利用及森林资源保护的方针、政策和法规；
4. Familiar with guidelines, policies and regulations on the use and protection of wildlife and forest resource protection;

5. 了解国内外野生动物学科、保护生物学学科的理论前沿、应用前景及发展动态。
5. Understand the theoretical frontier, prospects and development trends of domestic and foreign wildlife disciplines and conservation biology disciplines.

四、主要课程
Ⅳ. Main Courses

动物学、动物生态学、动物行为学、野生动物管理、自然保护管理、保护生物学、野生动物繁殖、野生动物饲养、野生动物疾病防治、野生动物保护、繁殖综合训练、毕业实习等。

Zoology, Animal Ecology, Ethology, Wildlife Management, Nature Conservation Management, Conservation Biology, Wildlife Breeding, Wildlife Domestication, Wildlife Disease Prevention, Wildlife Conservation, Breeding Comprehensive Training, Graduation Practice, etc.

（资料来源：百度百科 . http://baike.baidu.com/view/3353846.htm?fr=aladdin#2）

(Source: Baidu Encyclopedia. http://baike.baidu.com/view/3353846.htm?fr=aladdin#2)

主要参考文献
Main References

[1] 陈鹏 . 生物地理学 [M]. 长春：东北师范大学出版社，1989.

[1] CHEN Peng. Biogeography[M]. Changchun: Northeast Normal University Press, 1989.

[2] 马建章 , 邹红菲 , 贾竞波 . 野生动物管理学 [M]. 哈尔滨：东北林业大学出版社， 2004.

[2] MA Jianzhang, ZOU Hongfei, JIA Jingbo. Wildlife Management[M]. Harbin: Northeast Forestry   University Press, 2004.

[3] 张恒庆 , 张文辉 . 保护生物学 [M]. 2 版 . 北京：科学出版社，2009.

[3] ZHANG Hengqing, ZHANG Wenhui. Conservation Biology[M]. 2nd ed. Beijing: Science Press, 2009.

[4] 李俊清 . 保护生物学 [M]. 北京：科学出版社，2012.

[4] LI Junqing. Conservation Biology[M]. Beijing: Science Press, 2012.

注：本书部分图片来源于网络，因无法查找到作者，在此谨致谢意，请相关图片作者见到本书后与北京第二外国语学院附属中学联系。

Note: Some of the pictures in this book are taken from the Internet. Without access to the photographers, we hereby express our gratitude. Photographers of these pictures may contact The High School Affiliated to Beijing International Studies University after reading the book.

附录 1
Appendix I

中华人民共和国野生动物保护法
The Law of the People's Republic of China on the Protection of Wildlife

中华人民共和国野生动物保护法（全文）
Law of the People's Republic of China on the Protection of Wildlife (Full Text)

（1988 年 11 月 8 日第七届全国人民代表大会常务委员会第四次会议通过，根据 2004 年 8 月 28 日第十届全国人民代表大会常务委员会第十一次会议《关于修改〈中华人民共和国野生动物保护法〉的决定》修正）

(Adopted at the Fourth Meeting of the Standing Committee of the Seventh National People's Congress on November 8, 1988, and revised according to the *Decision on Revising the Law of the People's Republic of China on the Protection of Wildlife* made at the Eleventh Meeting of the Standing Committee of the Tenth National People's Congress on August 28, 2004)

第一章　总则
Chapter I　General Provisions

第一条　为保护、拯救珍贵、濒危野生动物，保护、发展和合理利用野生动物资源，维护生态平衡，制定本法。

Article 1　This Law is formulated for the purpose of protecting and saving the species of wildlife which are rare or near extinction, protecting, developing and rationally utilizing wildlife resources and maintaining ecological balances.

第二条　在中华人民共和国境内从事野生动物的保护、驯养繁殖、开发利用活动，必须遵守本法。

Article 2　All activities within the territory of the People's Republic of China concerning the protection, domestication, breeding, development and utilization of species of wildlife must be conducted in conformity with this Law.

本法规定保护的野生动物，是指珍贵、濒危的陆生、水生野生动物和有益的或者有重要经济、科学研究价值的陆生野生动物。

The wildlife protected under this Law refers to the species of terrestrial and aquatic wildlife which are rare or near extinction and the species of terrestrial wildlife which are beneficial or of important economic or scientific value.

本法各条款所提野生动物，均系指前款规定的受保护的野生动物。

The wildlife referred to in the provisions of this Law means the wildlife which shall enjoy protection as prescribed in the preceding paragraph.

珍贵、濒危的水生野生动物以外的其他水生野生动物的保护，适用渔业法的规定。

As regards the protection of the species of aquatic wildlife other than those which are rare or near extinction, the provisions of the Fisheries Law shall apply.

第三条　野生动物资源属于国家所有。

Article 3 Wildlife resources shall be owned by the State.

国家保护依法开发利用野生动物资源的单位和个人的合法权益。

The State shall protect the lawful rights and interests of units and individuals engaged in the development or utilization of wildlife resources according to law.

第四条　国家对野生动物实行加强资源保护、积极驯养繁殖、合理开发利用的方针，鼓励开展野生动物科学研究。

Article 4 The State shall pursue a policy of strengthening the protection of wildlife resources, actively domesticating and breeding the species of wildlife, and rationally developing and utilizing wildlife resources, and encourage scientific research on wildlife.

在野生动物资源保护、科学研究和驯养繁殖方面成绩显著的单位和个人，由政府给予奖励。

Units and individuals that have made outstanding achievements in the protection of wildlife resources, in scientific research on wildlife, or in the domestication and breeding of wildlife shall be awarded by the State.

第五条　中华人民共和国公民有保护野生动物资源的义务，对侵占或者破坏野生动物资源的行为有权检举和控告。

Article 5 Citizens of the People's Republic of China shall have the duty to protect wildlife resources and the right to inform the authorities of or file charges against acts of seizure or destruction of wildlife resources.

第六条　各级政府应当加强对野生动物资源的管理，制定保护、发展和合理利用野生动物资源的规划和措施。

Article 6 The governments at various levels shall strengthen the administration of wildlife resources and formulate plans and measures for the protection, development and rational utilization of wildlife resources.

第七条　国务院林业、渔业行政主管部门分别主管全国陆生、水生野生动物管理工作。

Article 7 The departments of forestry and fishery administration under the State Council shall be respectively responsible for the nationwide administration of terrestrial and aquatic wildlife.

省、自治区、直辖市政府林业行政主管部门主管本行政区域内陆生野生动物管理工作。自治州、县和市政府陆生野生动物管理工作的行政主管部门，由省、自治区、直辖市政府确定。

The departments of forestry administration under the governments of provinces, autonomous regions and municipalities directly under the Central Government shall be responsible for the administration of terrestrial wildlife in their respective areas. The departments in charge of the administration of terrestrial wildlife under the governments of autonomous prefectures, counties and municipalities shall be designated by the governments of provinces, autonomous regions or municipalities directly under the Central Government.

县级以上地方政府渔业行政主管部门主管本行政区域内水生野生动物管理工作。

The departments of fishery administration under the local governments at or above the county level shall be responsible for the administration of aquatic wildlife in their respective areas.

第二章　野生动物保护
Chapter II Protection of Wildlife

第八条　国家保护野生动物及其生存环境，禁止任何单位和个人非法猎捕或者破坏。

Article 8 The State shall protect wildlife and the environment for its survival, and shall prohibit the illegal hunting, catching or destruction of wildlife by any unit or individual.

第九条　国家对珍贵、濒危的野生动物实行重点保护。国家重点保护的野生动物分为一级保护野生动物和二级保护野生动物。国家重点保护的野生动物名录及其调整，由国务院野生动物行政主管部门制定，报国务院批准公布。

Article 9 The State shall give special protection to the species of wildlife which are rare or near extinction. The wildlife under special state protection shall consist of two classes: wildlife under first class protection and wildlife under second class protection. Lists or revised lists of wildlife under special state protection shall be drawn up by the department of wildlife administration under the State Council and announced after being submitted to and approved by the State Council.

地方重点保护野生动物，是指国家重点保护野生动物以外，由省、自治区、直辖市重点保护的野生动物。地方重点保护的野生动物名录，由省、自治区、直辖市政府制定并公布，报国务院备案。

The wildlife under special local protection, being different from the wildlife under special state protection, refers to the wildlife specially protected by provinces, autonomous regions or municipalities directly under the Central Government. Lists of wildlife under special local protection shall be drawn up and announced by the governments of provinces, autonomous regions or municipalities directly under the Central Government and shall be submitted to the State Council for the record.

国家保护的有益的或者有重要经济、科学研究价值的陆生野生动物名录及其调整，由国务院野生动物行政主管部门制定并公布。

Lists or revised lists of terrestrial wildlife under state protection, which are beneficial or of important economic or scientific value, shall be drawn up and announced by the department of wildlife administration under the State Council.

第十条 国务院野生动物行政主管部门和省、自治区、直辖市政府，应当在国家和地方重点保护野生动物的主要生息繁衍的地区和水域，划定自然保护区，加强对国家和地方重点保护野生动物及其生存环境的保护管理。

Article 10 The department of wildlife administration under the State Council and governments of provinces, autonomous regions and municipalities directly under the Central Government shall, in the main districts and water areas where wildlife under special state or local protection lives and breeds, designate nature reserves and strengthen the protection and administration of wildlife under special state or local protection and the environment for its survival.

自然保护区的划定和管理，按照国务院有关规定办理。

The designation and administration of nature reserves shall be effected in accordance with the relevant provisions of the State Council.

第十一条 各级野生动物行政主管部门应当监视、监测环境对野生动物的影响。

由于环境影响对野生动物造成危害时，野生动物行政主管部门应当会同有关部门进行调查处理。

Article 11 Departments of wildlife administration at various levels shall keep watch on and monitor the impact of the environment on wildlife. If the environmental impact causes harm to wildlife, the departments of wildlife administration shall conduct investigation and deal with the matter jointly with the departments concerned.

第十二条 建设项目对国家或者地方重点保护野生动物的生存环境产生不利影响的，建设单位应当提交环境影响报告书；环境保护部门在审批时，应当征求同级野生动物行政主管部门的意见。

Article 12 If a construction project produces adverse effects on the environment for the survival of wildlife under special state or local protection, the construction unit shall submit a report on the environmental impact. The department of environmental protection shall, in examining and approving the report, seek the opinion of the department of wildlife administration at the same level.

第十三条 国家和地方重点保护野生动物受到自然灾害威胁时，当地政府应当及时采取拯救措施。

Article 13 If natural disasters present threats to wildlife under special state or local protection, the local governments shall take timely measures to rescue them.

第十四条 因保护国家和地方重点保护野生动物，造成农作物或者其他损失的，由当地政府给予补偿。补偿办法由省、自治区、直辖市政府制定。

Article 14 If the protection of wildlife under special state or local protection causes losses to crops or other losses, the local governments shall make compensation for them. Measures for such compensation shall be formulated by the governments of provinces, autonomous regions and municipalities directly under the Central Government.

第三章 野生动物管理
Chapter III Administration of Wildlife

第十五条 野生动物行政主管部门应当定期组织对野生动物资源的调查，建立野生动物资源档案。

Article 15 The departments of wildlife administration shall regularly carry out surveys of wildlife resources and keep records of them.

第十六条 禁止猎捕、杀害国家重点保护野生动物。因科学研究、驯养繁殖、展览或者其他特殊情况，需要捕捉、捕捞国家一级保护野生动物的，必须向国务院野生动物行政主管部门申请特许猎捕证；猎捕国家二级保护野生动物的，必须向省、自治区、直辖市政府野生动物行政主管部门申请特许猎捕证。

Article 16 The hunting, catching or killing of wildlife under special state protection shall be prohibited. Where the catching or fishing of wildlife under first class state protection is necessary for scientific research, domestication and breeding, exhibition or other special purposes, the unit concerned must apply to the department of wildlife administration under the State Council for a special hunting and catching license; where the catching or hunting of wildlife under second class state protection is intended, the unit concerned must apply to the relevant department of wildlife administration under the government of a province, an autonomous region or a municipality directly under the Central Government for a special hunting and catching license.

第十七条　国家鼓励驯养繁殖野生动物。

Article 17 The State shall encourage the domestication and breeding of wildlife.

驯养繁殖国家重点保护野生动物的，应当持有许可证。许可证的管理办法由国务院野生动物行政主管部门制定。

Anyone who intends to domesticate and breed wildlife under special state protection shall obtain a license. Administrative measures for such licenses shall be formulated by the department of wildlife administration under the State Council.

第十八条　猎捕非国家重点保护野生动物的，必须取得狩猎证，并且服从猎捕量限额管理。

Article 18 Anyone who intends to hunt or catch wildlife that is not under special state protection must obtain a hunting license and observe the hunting quota assigned.

持枪猎捕的，必须取得县、市公安机关核发的持枪证。

Anyone who intends to hunt with a gun must obtain a gun license from the public security organ of the county or municipality concerned.

第十九条　猎捕者应当按照特许猎捕证、狩猎证规定的种类、数量、地点和期限进行猎捕。

Article 19 Anyone engaged in the hunting or catching of wildlife shall observe the prescriptions in his special hunting and catching license or his hunting license with respect to the species, quantity, area and time limit.

第二十条　在自然保护区、禁猎区和禁猎期内，禁止猎捕和其他妨碍野生动物生息繁衍的活动。

Article 20 In nature reserves and areas closed to hunting, and during seasons closed to hunting, the hunting and catching of wildlife and other activities which are harmful to the living and breeding of wildlife shall be prohibited.

禁猎区和禁猎期以及禁止使用的猎捕工具和方法，由县级以上政府或者其野生动物行政主管部门规定。

The areas and seasons closed to hunting as well as the prohibited hunting gear and methods shall be specified by governments at or above the county level or by the departments of wildlife administration under them.

第二十一条　禁止使用军用武器、毒药、炸药进行猎捕。

Article 21 The hunting or catching of wildlife by the use of military weapons, poison or explosives shall be prohibited.

猎枪及弹具的生产、销售和使用管理办法，由国务院林业行政主管部门会同公安部门制定，报国务院批准施行。

Measures for the control of the production, sale and use of hunting rifles and bullets shall be formulated by the department of forestry administration under the State Council jointly with the public security department, and shall enter into force after being submitted to and approved by the State Council.

第二十二条　禁止出售、收购国家重点保护野生动物或者其产品。因科学研究、驯养繁殖、展览等特殊情况，需要出售、收购、利用国家一级保护野生动物或者其产品的，必须经国务院野生动物行政主管部门或者其授权的单位批准；需要出售、收购、利用国家二级保护野生动物或者其产品的，必须经省、自治区、直辖市政府野生动物行政主管部门或者其授权的单位批准。

Article 22 The sale and purchase of wildlife under special state protection or the products thereof shall be prohibited. Where the sale, purchase or utilization of wildlife under first class state protection or the products thereof is necessary for scientific research, domestication and breeding, exhibition or other special purposes, the unit concerned must apply for approval by the department of wildlife administration under the State Council or by a unit authorized by the same department. Where the sale, purchase or utilization of wildlife under second class state protection or the products thereof is necessary, the unit concerned must apply for approval by the department of wildlife administration under the government of the relevant province, autonomous region or municipality directly under the Central Government or by a unit authorized by the same department.

驯养繁殖国家重点保护野生动物的单位和个人可以凭驯养繁殖许可证向政府指定的收购单位，按照规定出售国家重点保护野生动物或者其产品。

Units and individuals that domesticate and breed wildlife under special state protection may, by presenting their domestication and breeding licenses, sell wildlife under special state protection or the products thereof, in accordance with the relevant regulations, to purchasing units designated by the government.

工商行政管理部门对进入市场的野生动物或者其产品，应当进行监督管理。

The administrative authorities for industry and commerce shall exercise supervision and control over wildlife or the products thereof that are placed on the market.

第二十三条　运输、携带国家重点保护野生动物或者其产品出县境的，必须经省、自治区、直辖市政府野生动物行政主管部门或者其授权的单位批准。

Article 23　The transportation or carrying of wildlife under special state protection or the products thereof out of any county must be approved by the department of wildlife administration under the government of the relevant province, autonomous region or municipality directly under the Central Government, or by a unit authorized by the same department.

第二十四条　出口国家重点保护野生动物或者其产品的，进出口中国参加的国际公约所限制进出口的野生动物或者其产品的，必须经国务院野生动物行政主管部门或者国务院批准，并取得国家濒危物种进出口管理机构核发的允许进出口证明书。海关凭允许进出口证明书查验放行。

Article 24　The export of wildlife under special state protection or the products thereof, and the import or export of wildlife or the products thereof, whose import or export is restricted by international conventions to which China is a party, must be approved by the department of wildlife administration under the State Council or by the State Council, and an import or export permit must be obtained from the state administrative organ in charge of the import and export of the species which are near extinction. The Customs shall clear the imports or exports after examining the import or export permit.

涉及科学技术保密的野生动物物种的出口，按照国务院有关规定办理。

The export of the species of wildlife involving scientific and technological secrets shall be dealt with in accordance with relevant provisions of the State Council.

第二十五条　禁止伪造、倒卖、转让特许猎捕证、狩猎证、驯养繁殖许可证和允许进出口证明书。

Article 25 The forgery, sale or resale or transfer of special hunting and catching licenses, hunting licenses, domestication and breeding licenses, and import and export permits shall be prohibited.

第二十六条　外国人在中国境内对国家重点保护野生动物进行野外考察或者在野外拍摄电影、录像，必须经国务院野生动物行政主管部门或者其授权的单位批准。

Article 26 Where any foreigner intends, in the territory of China, to make surveys of or to film or videotape wildlife under special state protection in the field, he must apply for approval by the department of wildlife administration under the State Council or by a unit authorized by the same department.

建立对外国人开放的猎捕场所，必须经国务院野生动物行政主管部门批准。

The establishment of hunting grounds open to foreigners must be approved by the department of wildlife administration under the State Council.

第二十七条　经营利用野生动物或者其产品的，应当缴纳野生动物资源保护管理费。收费标准和办法由国务院野生动物行政主管部门会同财政、物价部门制定，报国务院批准后施行。

Article 27 Anyone engaged in the utilization of wildlife or the products thereof shall pay a fee for the protection and administration of wildlife resources. The schedule of the fee and the procedure for collecting, it shall be formulated by the department of wildlife administration under the State Council jointly with the financial and pricing authorities and shall enter into force after being submitted to and approved by the State Council.

第二十八条　因猎捕野生动物造成农作物或者其他损失的，由猎捕者负责赔偿。

Article 28 Anyone who has caused losses to crops or other losses while hunting or catching wildlife shall be held responsible for compensation.

第二十九条　有关地方政府应当采取措施，预防、控制野生动物所造成的危害，保障人畜安全和农业、林业生产。

Article 29 The local governments concerned shall take measures to prevent and control the harm caused by wildlife so as to guarantee the safety of human beings and livestock and ensure agricultural and forestry production.

第三十条　地方重点保护野生动物和其他非国家重点保护野生动物的管理办法，

由省、自治区、直辖市人民代表大会常务委员会制定。

Article 30 The administrative measures for wildlife under special local protection and for other wildlife that is not under special state protection shall be formulated by the standing committees of the people's congresses of provinces, autonomous regions and municipalities directly under the Central Government.

第四章 法律责任
Chapter Ⅳ Legal Responsibility

第三十一条 非法捕杀国家重点保护野生动物的，依照关于惩治捕杀国家重点保护的珍贵、濒危野生动物犯罪的补充规定追究刑事责任。

Article 31 Anyone who illegally catches or kills wildlife under special state protection shall be prosecuted for criminal responsibility in accordance with the supplementary provisions on punishing the crimes of catching or killing the species of wildlife under special state protection which are rare or near extinction.

第三十二条 违反本法规定，在禁猎区、禁猎期或者使用禁用的工具、方法猎捕野生动物的，由野生动物行政主管部门没收猎获物、猎捕工具和违法所得，处以罚款；情节严重、构成犯罪的，依照刑法第一百三十条的规定追究刑事责任。

Article 32 If anyone, in violation of the provisions of this Law, hunts or catches wildlife in an area or during a season closed to hunting or uses prohibited hunting gear or methods for the purpose, his catch, hunting gear and unlawful income shall be confiscated and he shall be fined by the department of wildlife administration; if the circumstances are serious enough to constitute a crime, he shall be prosecuted for criminal responsibility in accordance with the provisions of Article 130 of the Criminal Law.

第三十三条 违反本法规定，未取得狩猎证或者未按狩猎证规定猎捕野生动物的，由野生动物行政主管部门没收猎获物和违法所得，处以罚款，并可以没收猎捕工具，吊销狩猎证。

Article 33 If anyone, in violation of the provisions of this Law, hunts or catches wildlife without a hunting license or in violation of the prescriptions of the hunting license, his catch and unlawful income shall be confiscated and he shall be fined by the department of wildlife administration and, in addition, his hunting gear may be confiscated and his hunting license revoked.

违反本法规定，未取得持枪证持枪猎捕野生动物的，由公安机关比照治安管理处罚条例的规定处罚。

If anyone, in violation of the provisions of this Law, hunts wildlife with a hunting rifle without a license for the rifle, he shall be punished by a public security organ by applying mutatis mutandis the provisions of the Regulations on Administrative Penalties for Public Security.

第三十四条 违反本法规定，在自然保护区、禁猎区破坏国家或者地方重点保护野生动物主要生息繁衍场所的，由野生动物行政主管部门责令停止破坏行为，限期恢复原状，处以罚款。

Article 34 If anyone, in violation of the provisions of this Law, destroys in nature reserves or areas closed to hunting the main places where wildlife under special state or local protection lives and breeds, he shall be ordered by the department of wildlife administration to stop his destructive acts and restore these places to their original state within a prescribed time limit, and shall be fined.

第三十五条 违反本法规定，出售、收购、运输、携带国家或者地方重点保护野生动物或者其产品的，由工商行政管理部门没收实物和违法所得，可以并处罚款。

Article 35 If anyone, in violation of the provisions of this Law, sells, purchases, transports or carries wildlife under special state or local protection or the products thereof, such wildlife and products and his unlawful income shall be confiscated by the administrative authorities for industry and commerce and he may concurrently be fined.

违反本法规定，出售、收购国家重点保护野生动物或者其产品，情节严重、构成投机倒把罪、走私罪的，依照刑法有关规定追究刑事责任。

If anyone, in violation of the provisions of this Law, sells or purchases wildlife under special state protection or the products thereof, and if the circumstances are serious enough to constitute a crime of speculation or smuggling, he shall be prosecuted for criminal responsibility according to the relevant provisions of the Criminal Law.

没收的实物，由野生动物行政主管部门或者其授权的单位按照规定处理。

The wildlife or the products thereof thus confiscated shall, in accordance with the relevant provisions, be disposed of by the relevant department of wildlife administration or by a unit authorized by the same department.

第三十六条 非法进出口野生动物或者其产品的，由海关依照海关法处罚；情节严重、构成犯罪的，依照刑法关于走私罪的规定追究刑事责任。

Article 36 If anyone illegally imports or exports wildlife or the products thereof, he shall be punished by the Customs according to the Customs Law; if the circumstances are serious enough to constitute a crime, he shall be prosecuted for criminal responsibility in accordance with the provisions of the Criminal Law on the crimes of smuggling.

第三十七条　伪造、倒卖、转让特许猎捕证、狩猎证、驯养繁殖许可证或者允许进出口证明书的，由野生动物行政主管部门或者工商行政管理部门吊销证件，没收违法所得，可以并处罚款。

Article 37　If anyone forges, sells or resells or transfers a special hunting and catching license, a hunting license, a domestication and breeding license, or an import or export permit, his license or permit shall be revoked and his unlawful income shall be confiscated and he may concurrently be fined by the relevant department of wildlife administration or the administrative authorities for industry and commerce.

伪造、倒卖特许猎捕证或者允许进出口证明书，情节严重、构成犯罪的，比照刑法第一百六十七条的规定追究刑事责任。

If anyone who forges or sells or resells a special hunting and catching license or an import or export permit, and if the circumstances are serious enough to constitute a crime, he shall be prosecuted for criminal responsibility by applying mutatis mutandis the provisions of Article 167 of the Criminal Law.

第三十八条　野生动物行政主管部门的工作人员玩忽职守、滥用职权、徇私舞弊的，由其所在单位或者上级主管机关给予行政处分；情节严重、构成犯罪的，依法追究刑事责任。

Article 38　Any staff member of a department of wildlife administration who neglects his duty, abuses his power or engages in malpractices for personal gains shall be subject to administrative sanctions by the department to which he belongs or by the competent authority at a higher level; if the circumstances are serious enough to constitute a crime, he shall be prosecuted for criminal responsibility according to law.

第三十九条　当事人对行政处罚决定不服的，可以在接到处罚通知之日起十五日内，向作出处罚决定机关的上一级机关申请复议；对上一级机关的复议决定不服的，可以在接到复议决定通知之日起十五日内，向法院起诉。当事人也可以在接到处罚通知之日起十五日内，直接向法院起诉。当事人逾期不申请复议或者不向法院起诉又不履行处罚决定的，由作出处罚决定的机关申请法院强制执行。

Article 39　Any party who is dissatisfied with the decision on an administrative sanction may, within 15 days of receiving the notification on the sanction, make a request for reconsideration to the authority at the level next higher to the one that made the decision on the sanction; if he is dissatisfied with the decision on reconsideration made by the authority at the next higher level, he may, within 15 days of receiving the notification on the decision on reconsideration, institute legal proceedings in the court. The party may also directly institute legal proceedings in the court within 15 days of receiving the notification on the sanction. If the party neither makes a request for reconsideration, nor institutes legal proceedings in the court, nor complies with the decision on the sanction, the authority that made the decision on the sanction shall request the court to effect a compulsory execution of the decision.

对海关处罚或者治安管理处罚不服的，依照海关法或者治安管理处罚条例的规定办理。

If the party is dissatisfied with a Customs penalty or a penalty for violation of public security, the matter shall be dealt with in accordance with the provisions of the Customs Law or the Regulations on Administrative Penalties for Public Security.

第五章　附则
Chapter V　Supplementary Provisions

第四十条　中华人民共和国缔结或者参加的与保护野生动物有关的国际条约与本法有不同规定的，适用国际条约的规定，但中华人民共和国声明保留的条款除外。

Article 40　If any international treaty concerning the protection of wildlife, concluded or acceded to by the People's Republic of China, contains provisions differing from those of this Law, the provisions of the international treaty shall apply, unless the provisions are ones on which the People's Republic of China has made reservations.

第四十一条　国务院野生动物行政主管部门根据本法制定实施条例，报国务院批准施行。

Article 41　The department of wildlife administration under the State Council shall, in accordance with this Law, formulate regulations for its implementation which shall go into effect after being submitted to and approved by the State Council.

省、自治区、直辖市人民代表大会常务委员会可以根据本法制定实施办法。

The standing committees of the people's congresses of provinces, autonomous regions and municipalities directly under the Central Government may, in accordance with this Law, formulate measures for its implementation.

第四十二条　本法自 1989 年 3 月 1 日起施行。
Article 42　This Law shall come into force as of March 1, 1989.

附录 2
Appendix Ⅱ

国家重点保护野生动物名录
Lists of Wildlife under State Protection

（1988 年 12 月 10 日国务院批准）

(On December 10th,1988, the State Council for approval)

（注：2010 年有调整）

(Note:Adjusted in 2010)

中名	学名	保护级别	
		Ⅰ 级	Ⅱ 级
兽纲 MAMMALIA			
灵长目	PRIMATES		
懒猴科	Lorisldae		
蜂猴（所有种）	*Nycticebus* spp.	Ⅰ	
猴科	Cercopithecidae		
短尾猴	*Macaca arctoides*		Ⅱ
熊猴	*Macaca assamensis*	Ⅰ	
台湾猴	*Macaca cyclopis*	Ⅰ	
猕猴	*Macaca mulatta*		Ⅱ
豚尾猴	*Macaca nemestrina*	Ⅰ	
藏酋猴	*Macaca thibetana*		Ⅱ
叶猴（所有种）	*Presbytis* spp.	Ⅰ	
金丝猴（所有种）	*Rhinopithecus* spp.	Ⅰ	
猩猩科	Pongidae		
长臂猿（所有种）	*Hylobates* spp.	Ⅰ	
鳞甲目	PHOLIDOTA		
鲮鲤科	Manidae		
穿山甲	*Manis pentadactyla*		Ⅱ
食肉目	CARNIVORA		
犬科	Canidae		
豺	*Cuon alpinus*		Ⅱ

中名	学名	保护级别	
		I 级	II 级
熊科	Ursidae		
黑熊	*Selenarctos thibetanus*		II
棕熊（包括马熊）	*Ursus arctos (U.a. Pruinosus)*		II
马来熊	*Helarctas malayanus*	I	
浣熊科	Procyonidae		
小熊猫	*Ailurus fulgens*		II
大熊猫科	Ailuropodidae		
大熊猫	*Ailuropoda melanoleuca*	I	
鼬科	Mustelidae		
石貂	*Martes foina*		II
紫貂	*Martes zibellina*	I	
黄喉貂	*Martes flavigula*		II
貂熊	*Gulo gulo*	I	
*水獭（所有种）	*Lutra* spp.		II
*小爪水獭	*Aonyx cinerea*		II
灵猫科	Viverridae		
斑林狸	*Prionodon pardicolor*		II
大灵猫	*Viverra zibeiha*		II
小灵猫	*Viverricula indica*		II
熊狸	*Arctictis binturong*	I	
猫科	Felidae		
草原斑猫	*Felis lybica*(=*silvestris*)		II
荒漠猫	*Felis bieti*		II
丛林猫	*Felis chaus*		II
猞猁	*Lynx lynx*		II
兔狲	*Otocolobus manul*		II
金猫	*Catopuma temmincki*		II
渔猫	*Prionailurus viverrinus*		II
云豹	*Neojelis nebulosa*	I	
豹	*Panthera pardus*	I	
虎	*Panthera tigris*	I	
雪豹	*Panthera uncia*	I	
*鳍足目（所有种）	PINNIPEDIA		II
海牛目	SIRENIA		
儒艮科	Dugongidae		
*儒艮	*Dugong dugong*	I	

中名	学名	保护级别	
		I 级	II 级
鲸目	CETACEA		
喙豚科	Platanlstidae		
* 白鱀豚	*Lipotes vexillifer*	I	
海豚科	Delphinidae		
* 中华白海豚	*Sousa chinensis*	I	
* 其他鲸类	(Cetacea)		II
长鼻目	PROBOSCIDEA		
象科	Elephantidae		
亚洲象	*Elephas maximus*	I	
奇蹄目	PERISSODACTYLA		
马科	Equidae		
蒙古野驴	*Equus hemionus*	I	
西藏野驴	*Equus kiang*	I	
野马	*Equus przewalskii*	I	
偶蹄目	ARTIODACTYLA		
驼科	Camelidae		
野骆驼	*Camelus ferus* (=*bactrianus*)	I	
鼷鹿科	Tragulidae		
鼷鹿	*Tragulus javanicus*	I	
麝科	Moschidae		
麝（所有种）	*Moschus* spp.	I	
鹿科	Cervidae		
河麂	*Hydropotes inermis*		II
黑麂	*Muntiacus crinifrons*	I	
白唇鹿	*Cervus albirostris*	I	
马鹿（包括白臀鹿）	*Cervus elaphus* (C.e.*macneilli*)		II
坡鹿	*Cervus eldii*	I	
梅花鹿	*Cervus nippon*	I	
豚鹿	*Cervus porcinus*	I	
水鹿	*Cervus unicolor*		II
麋鹿	*Elaphurus davidianus*	I	
驼鹿	*Alces alces*		II
牛科	Bovidae		
野牛	*Bos gaurus*	I	

中名	学名	保护级别	
		Ⅰ级	Ⅱ级
野牦牛	*Bos mutus (=grunniens)*	Ⅰ	
黄羊	*Procapra gutturosa*		Ⅱ
普氏原羚	*Procapra przewalskii*	Ⅰ	
藏原羚	*Procapra picticaudata*		Ⅱ
鹅喉羚	*Cazella subgutturosa*		Ⅱ
藏羚	*Pantholops hodgsonii*	Ⅰ	
高鼻羚羊	*Saiga tatarica*	Ⅰ	
扭角羚	*Budorcas taxicolor*	Ⅰ	
鬣羚	*Capricornis sumatraensis*		Ⅱ
台湾鬣羚	*Capricornis crispus*	Ⅰ	
赤斑羚	*Naemorhedus cranbrooki*	Ⅰ	
斑羚	*Naemorhedus goral*		Ⅱ
塔尔羊	*Hemitragus jemlahicus*	Ⅰ	
北山羊	*Capra ibex*	Ⅰ	
岩羊	*Pseudois nayaur*		Ⅱ
盘羊	*Ovis ammon*		Ⅱ
兔形目	LAGOMORPHA		
兔科	Leporidae		
海南兔	*Lepus peguensis hainanus*		Ⅱ
雪兔	*Lepus timidus*		Ⅱ
塔里木兔	*Lepus yarkandensis*		Ⅱ
啮齿目	RODENTIA		
松鼠科	Sciuridae		
巨松鼠	*Ratufa bicolor*		Ⅱ
河狸科	Castoridae		
河狸	*Castor fiber*	Ⅰ	
鸟纲 AVES			
䴙䴘目	PODICIPEDIFORMES		
䴙䴘科	Podicipedidae		
角䴙䴘	*Podiceps auritus*		Ⅱ
赤颈䴙䴘	*Podiceps grisegena*		Ⅱ
鹱形目	PROCELLARIIFORMES		
信天翁科	Diomedeidae		
短尾信天翁	*Diomedea albatrus*	Ⅰ	

中名	学名	保护级别	
		I 级	II 级
鹈形目	PELECANIFORMES		
鹈鹕科	Pelecanidae		
鹈鹕（所有种）	*Pelecanus* spp.		II
鲣鸟科	Sulidae		
鲣鸟（所有种）	*Sula* spp.		II
鸬鹚科	Phalacrocoracidae		
海鸬鹚	*Phalacrocorax pelagicus*		II
黑颈鸬鹚	*Phalacrocorax niger*		II
军舰鸟科	Fregatidae		
白瓜军舰鸟	*Fregata andrewsi*	I	
鹳形目	CICONIIFORMES		
鹭科	Ardeidae		
黄嘴白鹭	*Egretta eulophotes*		II
岩鹭	*Egretta sacra*		II
海南虎斑鸦	*Gorsachius magnificus*		II
小苇鳽	*Ixbrychus minutus*		II
鹳科	Ciconiidae		
彩鹳	*Ibis leucocephalus*		II
白鹳	*Cicohio ciconia*	I	
黑鹳	*Ciconia nigra*	I	
鹮科	Threskiornithidae		
白鹮	*Threskiornis aethiopicus*		II
黑鹮	*Pseudibis papillosa*		II
朱鹮	*Nipponia Nippon*	I	
彩鹮	*Plegalis falcinellus*		II
白琵鹭	*Platalea leucorodia*		II
黑脸琵鹭	*Platalea minor*		II
雁形目	ANSERIFORMES		
鸭科	Anatidae		
红胸黑雁	*Branta ruficollis*		II
白额雁	*Anser albifrons*		II
天鹅（所有种）	*Cygnus* spp.		II
鸳鸯	*Aix galericulata*		II
中华秋沙鸭	*Mergus squamatus*	I	

中名	学名	保护级别	
		Ⅰ级	Ⅱ级
隼形目	FALCONIFORMES		
鹰科	Accipitridae		
金雕	*Aquila chrysaetos*	Ⅰ	
白肩雕	*Aquila heliaca*	Ⅰ	
玉带海雕	*Haliaeetus leucoryphus*	Ⅰ	
白尾海雕	*Haliaeetus albcilla*	Ⅰ	
虎头海雕	*Haliaeetus pelagicus*	Ⅰ	
拟兀鹫	*Pseudogyps bengalensis*	Ⅰ	
胡兀鹫	*Gypaetus barbatus*	Ⅰ	
其他鹰类	(Accipitridae)		Ⅱ
隼科（所有种）	Falconidae		Ⅱ
鸡形目	GALLIFORMES		
松鸡科	Tetraonidae		
细嘴松鸡	*Tetrao parvirostris*	Ⅰ	
黑琴鸡	*Lyrurus tetrix*		Ⅱ
柳雷鸟	*Lagopus lagopus*		Ⅱ
岩雷鸟	*Lagopus mutus*		Ⅱ
镰翅鸡	*Falcipennis falcipennis*		Ⅱ
花尾榛鸡	*Etrastes bonasla*		Ⅱ
斑尾榛鸡	*Etrastes sewerzowi*	Ⅰ	
雉科	Phasianidae		
雪鸡（所有种）	*Tetraogallus* spp.		Ⅱ
雉鹑	*Tetraophasis obscurus*	Ⅰ	
四川山鹧鸪	*ArboroPhila rufipectus*	Ⅰ	
海南山鹧鸪	*Arborophila ardens*	Ⅰ	
血雉	*Ithaginis cruentus*		Ⅱ
黑头角雉	*Tragopan melanocephalus*	Ⅰ	
红胸角雉	*Tragopan satyra*	Ⅰ	
灰腹角雉	*Tragopan blythii*	Ⅰ	
红腹角雉	*Tragopan temminchii*		Ⅱ
黄腹角雉	*Tragopan caboti*	Ⅰ	
虹雉（所有种）	*Lophophorus* spp.	Ⅰ	
藏马鸡	*Crossoptilon crossoptilon*		Ⅱ
蓝马鸡	*Crossoptilon aurtun*		Ⅱ

续表
Continued

中名	学名	保护级别	
		I 级	II 级
褐马鸡	*Crossoptilon mantchuricum*	I	
黑鹇	*Lophura leucomelana*		II
白鹇	*Lophura nycthemera*		II
蓝鹇	*Lophura swinhoii*	I	
原鸡	*Gallus gallus*		II
勺鸡	*Pucrasia macrolopha*		II
黑颈长尾雉	*Syrmaticus humiae*	I	
白冠长尾雉	*Syrmaticus reevesii*		II
白颈长尾雉	*Syrmaticus ewllioti*	I	
黑长尾雉	*Syrmaticus mikado*	I	
锦鸡（所有种）	*Chrysolophus* spp.		II
孔雀雉	*Polyplectron bicalcaratum*	I	
绿孔雀	*Pavo muticus*	I	
鹤形目	GRUIFORMES		
鹤科	Gruidae		
灰鹤	*Grus grus*		II
黑颈鹤	*Grum nigricollis*	I	
白头鹤	*Grus monacha*	I	
沙丘鹤	*Grus canadensis*		II
丹顶鹤	*Grus japonensis*	I	
白枕鸿	*Grus vipio*		II
白鹤	*Grus leucogeranus*	I	
赤颈鹤	*Grus antigone*	I	
蓑羽鹤	*Anthropoides virgo*		II
秧鸡科	Rallidae		
长脚秧鸡	*Crex crex*		II
姬田鸡	*Porzana parva*		II
棕背田鸡	*Porzana bicolor*		II
花田鸡	*Coturnicops noveboracensis*		II
鸨科	Otidae		
鸨（所有种）	*Otis* spp.	I	
鸻形目	CHARADRIIFORMES		
雉鸻科	Jacanidae		
铜翅水雉	*Metopidius indicus*		II

中名	学名	保护级别	
		Ⅰ级	Ⅱ级
鹬科	Soolopacidae		
小杓鹬	*Numenius borealis*		Ⅱ
小青脚鹬	*Tringa guttifer*		Ⅱ
燕鸻科	Glareolidae		
灰燕鸻	*Glareola lactea*		Ⅱ
鸥形目	LARIFORMES		
鸥科	Laridae		
遗鸥	*Larus relictus*	Ⅰ	
小鸥	*Larus minutus*		Ⅱ
黑浮鸥	*Chlidonias niger*		Ⅱ
黄嘴河燕鸥	*Sterna aurantia*		Ⅱ
黑嘴端凤头燕鸥	*Thalasseus zimmermanni*		Ⅱ
鸽形目	COLUMBIFORMES		
沙鸡科	Pteroclididae		
黑腹沙鸡	*Pterocles orientalis*		Ⅱ
鸠鸽科	Columbidae		
绿鸠（所有种）	*Treron* spp.		Ⅱ
黑颏果鸠	*Ptilinopus leclancheri*		Ⅱ
皇鸠（所有种）	*Ducula* spp.		Ⅱ
斑尾林鸽	*Columba palumbus*		Ⅱ
鹃鸠（所有种）	*Macropygia* spp.		Ⅱ
鹦形目	PSITTACIFORMES		
鹦鹉科（所有种）	Psittacidae		Ⅱ
鹃形目	CUCULIFORMES		
杜鹃科	Cuculidae		
鸦鹃（所有种）	*Centropus* spp.		Ⅱ
鸮形目（所有种）	STRIGIFORMES		Ⅱ
雨燕目	APODIFORMES		
雨燕科	Apodidae		
灰喉针尾雨燕	*Hirundapus cochinchinensls*		Ⅱ
凤头雨燕科	Hemiprocnidae		
凤头雨燕	*Hemiprocne longipennis*		Ⅱ
咬鹃目	TROGONIFORMES		
咬鹃科	Trogonidae		
橙胸咬鹃	*Harpactes oreskios*		Ⅱ

中名	学名	保护级别	
		I级	II级
佛法僧目	CORACIIFORMES		
翠鸟科	Alcedinidae		
蓝耳翠鸟	*Alcedo meninting*		II
鹳嘴翠鸟	*Pelargopsis capensis*		II
蜂虎科	Meropidae		
黑胸蜂虎	*Merops leschenaulti*		II
绿喉蜂虎	*Merops orientalis*		II
犀鸟科（所有种）	Bucertidae		II
鴷形目	PICIFORMES		
啄木鸟科	Picidae		
白腹黑啄木鸟	*Dryocopus javensis*		II
雀形目	PASSERIFORMES		
阔嘴鸟科（所有种）	Eurylaimidae		II
八色鸫科（所有种）	Pittidae		II
爬行纲 REPTILIA			
龟鳖目	TESTUDOFORMES		
龟科	Emydidae		
* 地龟	*Geoemyda spengleri*		II
* 三线闭壳龟	*Cuora trifasciata*		II
* 云南闭壳龟	*Cuora yunnanensis*		II
陆龟科	Testudinidae		
四爪陆龟	*Testudo horsfieldi*	I	
凹甲陆龟	*Manouria impressa*		II
海龟科	Cheloniidae		
* 蠵龟	*Caretta caretta*		II
* 绿海龟	*Chelonia mydas*		II
* 玳瑁	*Eretmochelys imbricata*		II
* 太平洋丽龟	*Lepidochelys olivacea*		II
棱皮龟科	Dermochelyidae		
* 棱皮龟	*Dermochelys coriacea*		II
鳖科	Trionychidae		
* 鼋	*Pelochelys bibroni*	I	
* 山瑞鳖	*Trionyx steindachneri*		II

中名	学名	保护级别	
		Ⅰ级	Ⅱ级
蜥蜴目	LACERTIFORMES		
壁虎科	Gekkonidae		
大壁虎	*Gekko gecko*		Ⅱ
鳄蜥科	Shinisauridae		
蜥鳄	*Shinisaurus crocodilurus*	Ⅰ	
巨蜥科	Varanidae		
巨蜥	*Varanus salvator*	Ⅰ	
蛇目	SERPENTIFORMES		
蟒科	Boidae		
蟒	*Python molurus*	Ⅰ	
鳄目	CROCODILIFORMES		
鼍科	Alligatoridae		
扬子鳄	*Alligator sinensis*	Ⅰ	
两栖纲 AMPHIBIA			
有尾目	CAUDATA		
隐鳃鲵科	Cryptobranchidae		
*大鲵	*Andrias davidianus*		Ⅱ
蝾螈科	Salamandridae		
*细痣疣螈	*Tylototriton asperrimus*		Ⅱ
*镇海疣螈	*Tylototriton chinhaiensis*		Ⅱ
*贵州疣螈	*Tylototriton kweichowensis*		Ⅱ
*大凉疣螈	*Tylototriton taliangensis*		Ⅱ
*细瘰疣螈	*Tylototriton verrucosus*		Ⅱ
无尾目	ANURA		
蛙科	Ranidae		
虎纹蛙	*Rana tigrina*		Ⅱ
鱼纲 PISCES			
鲈形目	PERCIFORMES		
石首鱼科	Sciaenidae		
*黄唇鱼	*Bahaba flavolabiata*		Ⅱ
杜父鱼科	Cottidae		
*松江鲈鱼	*Trachidermus fasciatus*		Ⅱ
海龙鱼目	SYNGNATHIFORMES		
海龙鱼科	Syngnathidae		
*克氏海马鱼	*Hippocampus kelloggi*		Ⅱ

中名	学名	保护级别	
		I 级	II 级
鲤形目	CYPRINIFORMES		
胭脂鱼科	Catostomidae		
* 胭脂鱼	*Myxocyprinus asiaticus*		II
鲤科	Cyprinidae		
* 唐鱼	*Tanichthys albonubes*		II
* 大头鲤	*Cyprinus Pellegrini*		II
* 金线鲃	*Sinocyclocheilus grahami grahami*		II
* 新疆大头鱼	*Aspiorhynchus laticeps*	I	
* 大理裂腹鱼	*Schizothorax taliensis*		II
鳗鲡目	ANGUILLIFOMES		
鳗鲡科	Anguillidae	I	
* 花鳗鲡	*Anguilla marmorata*		II
鲑形目	SALMONIFORMES		
鲑科	Salmonidae		
* 川陕哲罗鲑	*Hucho bleekeri*		II
* 秦岭细鳞鲑	*Brachymystax lenok tsinlingensis*		II
鲟形目	ACIPENSERIFORMES		
鲟科	Acipenseridae		
* 中华鲟	*Acipenser sinensis*	I	
* 达氏鲟	*Acipenser dabryanus*	I	
匙吻鲟科	Polyodontidae		
* 白鲟	*Psephurus gladius*	I	
文昌鱼纲 APPENDICULARIA			
文昌鱼目	AMPHIOXIFORMES		
文昌鱼科	Branchiostomatidae		
* 文昌鱼	*Branchiotoma belcheri*		II
珊瑚纲 ANTHOZOA			
柳珊瑚目	GOKGONACEA		
红珊瑚科	Coralliidae		
* 红珊瑚	*Corallium* spp.	I	
腹足纲 GASTROPODA			
中腹足目	MESOGASTROPODA		
宝贝科	Cypraeidae		
* 虎斑宝贝	*Cypraea tigris*		II

中名	学名	保护级别	
		Ⅰ级	Ⅱ级
冠螺科	Cassididae		
*冠螺	*Cassis cornuta*		Ⅱ
瓣鳃纲 LAMELLIBRANCHIA			
异柱目	ANISOMYARIA		
珍珠贝科	Pteriidae		
*大珠母贝	*Pinctada maxima*		Ⅱ
真瓣鳃目	EULAMELLIBRANCHIA		
砗磲科	Tridacnidae		
*库氏砗磲	*Trldacna cookiana*	Ⅰ	
蚌科	Unionidae		
*佛耳丽蚌	*Lamprotula mansuyi*		Ⅱ
头足纲 UEPHALOPODA			
四鳃目	TETRABRANCHIA		
鹦鹉螺科	Nautilidae		
*鹦鹉螺	*Nautilus pompilius*	Ⅰ	
昆虫纲 INSECTA			
双尾目	UIPLURA		
蛱虫八科	Japygidae		
伟蛱虫八	*Atlasjapyx atlas*		Ⅱ
蜻蜓目	ODONATA		
箭蜓科	Gomphidae		
尖板曦箭蜓	*Heliogomphus retroflexus*		Ⅱ
宽纹北箭蜓	*Ophiogomphus spinicorne*		Ⅱ
缺翅目	ZORAPTERA		
缺翅虫科	Zorotypidae		
中华缺翅虫	*Zorotypus sinensis*		Ⅱ
墨脱缺翅虫	*Zorotypus medoensis*		Ⅱ
蛩蠊目	GRYLLOBLATTODAE		
蛩蠊科	Grylloblattidae		
中华蛩蠊	*Galloisiana sinensls*	Ⅰ	

中名	学名	保护级别	
		I 级	II 级
鞘翅目	**COLEOPTERA**		
步甲科	Carabidae		
拉步甲	*Carabus (Coptolabrus) lafossei*		II
硕步甲	*Carabus (Apotopterus) davidi*		II
臂金龟科	Euchitldae		
彩臂金龟（所有种）	*Cheirotonus* spp.		II
犀金龟科	Dynastidae		
叉犀金龟	*Allomyrina davidis*		II
鳞翅目	**LEPIDOPTERA**		
凤蝶科	Papilionidae		
金斑喙凤蝶	*Teinopalpus aureus*	I	
双尾褐凤蝶	*Bhutanitis mansfieldi*		II
三尾褐凤蝶	*Bhutanitis thaidina dongchuanensls*		II
中华虎凤蝶	*Lueddorfia chinensis huashanensis*		II
绢蝶科	Parnassidae		
阿波罗绢蝶	*Parnassius apollo*		II
	肠鳃纲 ENTEROPNEUSTA		
柱头虫科	Balanoglossidae		
*多鳃孔舌形虫	*Glossobalanus polybranchioporus*	I	
玉钩虫科	Harrlmaniidae		
*黄岛长吻虫	*Saccoglossus hwangtauensis*	I	